Wonderful Ways
to Love a Teen

Wonderful Ways
to Love a Teen

... Even When It Seems Impossible

Judy Ford

Conari Press
Berkeley, CA

Printed in the United States of America on recycled paper
Cover Design and Illustration: Kathy Warriner

Conari Press books are distributed by Publishers Group West

Library of Congress Cataloging-in-Publication Data

Ford, Judy, 1944-
Wonderful ways to love a teen : —even when it seems impossible / Judy Ford.
   p.   cm.
ISBN 1-57324-023-0 (trade paper)
   1. Parent and teenager.   2. Parenting.   3. Youth—Family relationships.
4. Adolescent psychology.
HQ799.15.F67   1996   95-496442
649'.125—dc20   CIP

3 4 5 6 7 8 9 0

For some of my favorite teens:

Amanda, Chuck, Stephanie,
Sara, Jayme,
Derek, Josh, and Greg,
you delight and surprise me.

Acknowledgments

To my brilliant friends at Conari Press—Mary Jane, Will, Emily, and Erin—for treating me royally and adding so much excitement to my year.

Cheers to my friends Jean Gabriella and George, Regina and Rodney. You're shining examples of what it means to parent teens—as they say, the proof is in the pudding.

To Chloe, Dave, Patricia, and Shari, for the comfort of your friendship.

Thank you all.

Wonderful Ways
to Love a Teen

Spirit

Security

The Art of Relating

The ideal parents know they don't know everything.

When I mentioned to people that I was writing a sequel to *Wonderful Ways to Love a Child* called *Wonderful Ways to Love a Teen*, they rolled their eyes and said, "We sure can use that book!" or they would laugh, shake their heads in disbelief, and ask, "Is it possible?"

Then I would ask them, "Do you love your teenager?" And without exception these very same people would answer, "Yes, of course!" And as they complained about their son or daughter, I'd see a sparkle in their eye and an undefined grace softening their face. As a cab driver in Dallas, the father of two teenage girls, said, "They are the spring in my step."

In my years of counseling and teaching, I've talked with thousands of parents who love their teenagers but aren't sure how to show it. They want to have a positive relationship but they're uncertain of their role, and they wonder if their teenager still needs them. And because they don't know what to do, misunderstandings pile up, hurt and anger accumulate, and the distance between parent and child grows.

The idea that teenagers are impossible to talk to, live with, and relate to has become so commonplace that we adults start to believe and act as if it's so. The myth of the difficult teenage years is perpetuated over and over until everyone believes that all teenagers are difficult all the time. It just isn't so.

The teenage years run smoothly and joyously for some parents, whereas others find them impossible. Some parents savor every minute with their teenagers, knowing they'll soon be gone. Others find it so arduous to relate that they throw in the towel and withdraw—counting the days until their teenager moves out. Some parents find the relationship with their teenager so fulfilling—not only because they're learning the art of finesse and tact, but because the house is so lively—that there's excitement in the air. Still others resort to threats, punishment, and authoritarian rule to avoid relating.

Often, it seems that our teenagers do not want our love. The truth is that they do, but in a new way. However difficult it may feel sometimes, I am convinced that it is always better to strive for a conscious relationship with your teen—even during those times when you wonder if you're being stretched beyond your capabilities. That's because I truly believe—based on my own experience and my work with hundreds of parents—that if relating to your teenager is impossible, it's because you don't have the tools. Once you gain the tools, a relationship with a teenager is no more difficult than any other relationship. For the truth is that the teenage stage of life is no more difficult than any other stage of life; it just takes new skills.

Wonderful Ways to Love a Teen is a handbook of tools to guide you in the art of relating to your teenager. Even when your parent/teen relationship appears hopelessly beyond repair, you can follow its suggestions to help you rebuild a loving bond.

The first thing to understand is that the parenting skills we learned with our young children no longer apply—after all, it's much easier to parent a small child who thinks you're perfect than to relate to a teenager who is talking back, pointing out your faults, and pushing you away. Loving and parenting a teenager requires a more astute, subtle, sophisticated style. That's why relating to a teenager is an art that demands a more conscious approach to parenting, and, like with learning any other art form, you will gain the needed proficiency only with diligent practice. Over the next few years, you will have lots of opportunities to sharpen your style.

Parenting a teenager is the most intense course in the art of relating you could ever undertake. It's a extensive curriculum of compassion, communication, diplomacy, and conflict resolution—like being in an encounter group of sorts, where you learn more about yourself than your teenager and more about yourself than you really wanted to know. For twelve years, your child was your buddy, companion, and cheerful friend; and just when you think you have things under control, he or she turns thirteen, and you find out you really don't know for sure. Parenting a teen means you'll undoubtedly discover that you still have much to learn.

Over the years with a teen, you'll discover how patient and generous you can be—as well as how crazy and immature, and how low you can really sink. With a teenager in your life, you'll most certainly uncover your not-so-loving characteristics—your jealousy, your anger, your fear, your insecurities. You'll get discouraged and pull your hair out. At times, you'll scream in frustration, behave irrationally, and find your thoughts swirling in confusion. And although there's no escape, you won't be afflicted forever if you choose to grow, to hang in there, and uncover the teachings in whatever difficulties you face.

As a painter struggles with the canvas to get it just right, so will you struggle as you acquire the special knack of giving just the right amount of advice, encouragement, and counsel. If you are willing to keep learning, evolving, and maturing, you'll earn the privilege of watching a young adult emerge; then you can be deservedly proud.

The rewards are immeasurable. When eighteen-year-old Ellie left for college, she wrote this note to her parents: "I've always needed you and always will. Whoever I am, whatever I become, it's because I know you love me."

And so, parents of good heart who struggle so valiantly to learn these lessons, remember that your teenagers, although they may never say so, are counting on you!

Serenity

It's paradoxical that when
you're patient with your teen,
when you've stopped insisting,
and forcing, the very thing
you're hoping for can happen.

Expect the Unexpected

Parents who have successfully raised a teen know that this stage is full of ups and downs. It's like riding a roller coaster: even when you know the highs and lows are coming, you still get quite a jolt. One minute your daughter is acting so maturely that you have to blink to make sure this is still your child; the next minute she's pitching a fit like she did when she was two. And the worse thing is you never know which of the two personas will respond in any given situation.

Parenting involves a great amount of teaching. When your child was young, you taught him many things: how to dress himself, tie his shoes, brush his teeth, and ride a bicycle, as well as how to relate to others, and generally be a civilized human being. By the time he's a teenager, he'll be so capable and responsible that you might both forget he hasn't mastered everything.

There's a long list of things teens need to know from you—practical things such as how to apply for a job, drive a car, do the laundry, and fix a meal. They need lessons in money management, time management, and social skills. They also need to learn more intangible things, like how to lead a balanced, life and how to treat themselves and other people well. The underlying message in all you're conveying is *responsible freedom*. Together, all the things you're teaching add up to your giving your teenager more and more responsibility for his personal freedom. But his ability to bear this responsibility doesn't usually come about in an orderly progression. It's more of a one-step-forward-two-steps-back kind of thing.

Remember when you taught your son to tie his shoes? He didn't quite have the hang of it, but he tried to do it anyway; then he got frustrated when he couldn't do it the first time. When you tried to show him again, he got irritated, cried, and pushed you away. But you and he diligently kept at it until he got the hang of it.

It's the same with teens. They're ready to take on new freedoms and responsibilities even though they haven't mastered all the skills; and as you show them what they need to know, unexpectedly they'll get impatient and lash out. In the midst of this commotion, you will be called on to keep your wits about you. It's a big achievement to keep calm, but it's worth it. For just as she learned to cross the street, if you keep guiding, she'll learn to fly.

Laugh About Inconsistencies

Your teen can be a bundle of contradictions, one minute accusing you of interfering, and the next minute demanding your advice. Instead of pointing out the crazy inconsistencies, you'll feel calmer if you grin and have a good private laugh. Unless you can laugh to yourself about these unpredictable, unexplainable detours (laughing at them aloud is a no-no), you'll have some rough years ahead.

When my daughter, Amanda, was sixteen, she came home from school one day and I said cheerfully, "Hi, honey, how was your day?" To this she responded, "Just once I wish I could come home and you wouldn't say, 'Hi, honey, how was your day?' Just once I wish I could come home after a hard day at school to peace and quiet and not have to answer your questions." Wanting to be a responsive, caring parent, I listened carefully without talking back (the really hard part) and made a mental note of her request. The next day, I made sure I was in my room with the door closed so I wouldn't disturb her when she came home from school. To my astonishment, as she walked through the kitchen she yelled, "Mom, Mom, where are you?" And as she started telling me about her day, I thought to myself: It's confusing to live with a teenager.

Brittany wanted her mom to help her choose a prom dress, but each time her mother made suggestions Brittany said, "You know I don't like that color," or "You know I don't like that style. Why can't you help me find something I like?" Her mom felt perturbed, but since she understood that Brittany was feeling pressure to get just the perfect dress, she decided not to defend herself. Instead, she tried as best she could to do what Brittany wanted: "If you like that one, honey, let's get it. . . . Yes, that looks nice, too." She thought she was doing okay, when Brittany scolded, "Mom, I'd like some helpful feedback. Why aren't you telling me what you like?" She gave Brittany a questioning look that said, *Are you kidding*? They continued shopping, eventually agreeing on the long purple dress. Mom still doesn't know what happened, but she laughs about it.

These discrepancies are definitely not worth arguing about. Matthew says, "Some of the stupidest conversations I've had with my fifteen-year-old son are when I'm in my 'I'm right' mode, trying to point out his inconsistencies."

When you find yourself caught off guard by these little inconsistencies, you'll be better off ignoring most of them, shaking your head in disbelief, and keeping it to yourself. Better yet—share it with your spouse or another parent and have a good laugh. In fact, you'll probably be chuckling for years.

Choose Power Struggles Wisely

Inherent in living with your teenager is the potential for daily disagreements, frequent fights, major power struggles, and little rows and quarrels, so choose them carefully, cautiously, and mindfully.

What does it mean to choose your power struggles wisely? It means using your expertise to sidestep hassling over nonsense—small stuff that in the big scheme of things doesn't really matter much. When you have some life experience under your belt, you recognize that fighting over the small stuff is detrimental. Taking on battles just to prove who's the boss or who's right causes a lot of dissension, and is a bad example for your teenager.

"The day Carly turned thirteen we started fighting," her mother, Laura, told me. "I don't know what starts most of our fights. At the time it seems important, but the next day I feel horrid. I don't want to fight with her, but I get hooked every time." It's true that when you fight over the insignificant stuff such as hair, clothes, makeup, music, food, and the like, you'll both end up feeling bad—and there will be a gap between you. Such a big rumpus, mountains of hurt feelings, and nothing settled.

Just because you don't agree with everything your teenager is doing, you don't have to confront it. You can let some things slide because you know she'll learn, as you did, by trial and error. If you're going to have a confrontation, it's a good idea to understand clearly what you're trying to accomplish. Instead of shouting, lashing out, or handing down orders, a mature parent thinks about what action needs to be taken. Don't be a firecracker, going off without thinking of the consequences, by saying such things as: "You're old enough to know better." "As long as you are living under my roof . . ." "Because I said so, that's why." "When I was your age . . ."

Before you start pointing out how you want things done, ask yourself: Is this really worth all the friction and hard feelings it could cause? Is it worth putting distance and misunderstanding between me and my child one more time? Remember, that as the head of the household, you don't have to exert your authority by getting caught up in incessant arguing.

After raising two children and with a sixteen year old left at home, Sam said, "We don't fight about trivia anymore. We step in and take charge occasionally, but mostly we step back."

When you step back, you can let the insignificant pass while demonstrating a level of maturity that is good for your teen to see.

Take Time to Unwind

You thought childbirth was painful—some say it was a piece of cake compared to living with a teen. One thing is for sure: You'll need those childbirth skills of deep breathing in order to relax and get your bearings. Breathing helps you avoid that frenzied feeling; and when you're relaxed, you're better able to focus on the joys of watching your child grow up. When you're at ease, you're able to see how well you've done, what a fine young person you're raising. And when you're feeling tranquil, you're able to experience the bond with your child, the heart connection, the eternal link.

Parents and teens often feel so rushed that it's easy to forget to rest, unwind, and enjoy one another. You *want* to take it easy, you think about it, you intend to, but then schedules get jammed and the "to-do" list grows, so you put off slowing down until the weekend. Then chores and outside commitments take first priority, enjoying your family takes a backseat, and you're too busy to catch your breath.

Some parents tell me that weeks go by without their saying anything more then hello and good-bye to their teenagers, not because they haven't wanted to be with one another, but because their lives are loaded with demands and obligations. The years from junior high to high school can be one big blur. Soon the kids are graduating, and you barely remember what happened.

Our teenagers' lives get out of balance, too. Some kids take tough academic loads and spend every waking moment studying. Others pack their schedules so tightly with sports, work, and extracurricular activities that soon they're so busy they forget to smell the roses, taste the pizza, hear the music. They rush too fast to notice.

We don't want our teenagers soaking up the anxieties of this fast-paced life, but we don't know what to do. We get caught up in the pursuit of the goal, thinking that once they've made the team, the honor roll, or won a scholarship, they'll have it made—*then* they can start living—so we push our teenagers to achieve. Before you know it, they're overwhelmed too.

When your or your teenager's life lacks balance, it's time to simplify. You can simplify your life by avoiding making comparisons, by taking regular time for play, and by letting yourself and your teenager sit and stare—doing nothing is important, too. Wally, a grandfather of five teenagers, is known for his easygoing manner. He doesn't get ruffled when things go wrong. His motto is *Work hard and sit down when you're tired.* Good idea!

Give Them Reasons to Be Proud of You

You want to be proud of your teenager, and your teenager wants to be proud of you. She wants to look up to you as a person she admires. Just as she pleases you by the choices she makes, in the same way she will look at your life to determine whether or not she can respect you. Your teenager will love you because you're her parent, but if you want her to be proud of you, it is imperative that you conduct yourself with candor, goodness, and integrity.

Sharon was a smoker and yet she was appalled when she caught her thirteen-year-old daughter, Lydia, smoking on the street corner. "I can't believe it," she scolded. "You look so cheap, not to mention what it's doing to your health." Sharon nagged, threatened, and bribed Lydia to stop. Lydia offered, "I'll stop if you will, Mom." Sharon tried and failed. "I can't, it's too hard." Lydia hasn't stopped either.

You can't teach your adolescent to be truthful if you're living in denial about your own life. You can't teach her to be trustworthy if you don't keep your commitments. You can't teach her to make good decisions if you never give her a chance to decide for herself. You can't teach her to talk things through when you fly off the handle. If you are unhappy with yourself, you can't fake it—your teenager will see through your lies.

Unfortunately, too many teenagers grow up in spiritually bankrupt homes, living with parents who are alcoholic or physically or mentally abusive. Some teenagers live with rage and shame inflicted on them by parents who refuse to be accountable for their own lives or heal their personal pain.

Teenagers deserve to feel safe, valued, loved, and cared for by parents who, although not perfect, are living lives based on honesty, integrity, wisdom, and love—who practice what they preach.

Your children see you; they know who you are. They are watching your character. They can describe your traits, your personality, your disposition, and the stuff you are made of. What attributes, virtues, and qualities do you want them to see? Can they be proud of you?

Remember Your Own Feelings as a Teenager

Remember when you were in junior high and high school? What were you thinking and feeling? What was important to you? If you remember your adolescence, you're better equipped as a parent to find creative solutions to the dilemmas of living with your teen.

There can be a pitfall in remembering, however, as one dad told me: "I was really wild when I was my son's age—drinking, vandalizing, and stealing. At first I assumed that if I did it, my kid would, too, but as I thought about it, I realized our circumstances and surroundings are entirely different."

Although it is helpful to remember what you experienced and felt as an adolescent, you don't want to assume that your teenager is doing the same things. Don't assume that he has the same problems you did or that he'll handle them as you did. Your teenager isn't you. Actually, many parents brag that their kids are wiser and more competent than they were at the same age.

However, remembering your own experiences can go a long way toward maintaining empathy for your kids. What was life like for you as a teen? What do you wish could have been different? What changes would you make? How did you feel about your body when it started to change? What did you wish your parents would have understood? What was your relationship like with your parents? What kind of relationship do you have with them now? Did you wear bell bottoms? Have a flattop? Grow your hair to your shoulders? What was your favorite music? Did you like your looks? Were you popular? Teens have inner conflicts that are often too personal to share. Did you?

Forty-year-old Rebecca remembers, "In junior high, a classmate said I had a horse smile. I was mortified. From that moment on I decided to look dignified. I practiced smiling for hours in front of the mirror. I got so I knew how wide to smile. But sometimes I'd forget to give a sophisticated smile and when I'd see my picture, there I'd be with the ugly horse smile and I'd be so humiliated, I'd think: All these other kids have dignified, quiet smiles, why can't I?"

When you think back to your own adolescence, you'll remember how complex it really was and you'll be more compassionate toward your sons and daughters. And when you share with them what life was like for you, what self-doubts you had, they'll probably be more good-natured and benevolent toward you.

See Beyond the Obvious

Here is a true story told to me by Kathleen, a thirty-six-year-old mother of an eighteen-year-old girl: "When Hailey turned thirteen, I felt a real change in our relationship. For years she'd been my buddy; now we were arguing and not having much fun. She was pretty, popular, and smart; she had a room of her own—when I was her age, I shared mine with two older sisters. As a kid, I wore hand-me-downs, so I couldn't stand it when she threw her clothes on the floor. When she talked back, I threatened to take the phone away. If she didn't empty the garbage or do the dishes on time, I withheld her allowance. When boys started hanging around, I got stricter. I refused to let her go to any parties, and once when I saw her come out of a movie with boys from school, I grounded her.

"Things went downhill from there. I complained nonstop to my friends; they all agreed she was behaving badly. They told me horror stories about their own teenagers. My mother called her spoiled and said it was my fault. Hailey was upset and so was I. I was convinced there was nothing I could do and chalked our difficulties up to the 'teenage thing.' I was angry and jealous, but I didn't realize it at first.

"In spite of all the turmoil at home, in her senior year, Hailey was elected homecoming queen, sang with a local jazz group, made honor society, and received a college scholarship. On graduation night, the school counselor said to me, 'I can see your spirit and spunk in Hailey. Congratulations! She's who she is because of you.' That comment struck me like a lightening bolt, and right then I began to look at Hailey and myself in a new light.

"It was true, Hailey was bright, pretty, spirited. When I looked closely, I could see my same determination within her, and slowly I began to realize that I had blamed her for what I'd missed. She'd had the opportunities I'd wanted for myself, and instead of encouraging her, I focused on her shortcomings. I unconsciously blamed her for what I was missing. Slowly, I began to appreciate who I was, and my childhood wounds began to heal."

It's easy to blame teenagers for what's going wrong in our lives. After all, it's true they're more than slightly narcissistic. But when you look beyond the surface and probe a little deeper, you will find there's always something else going on. Often, like Kathleen, it's something within yourself that can use some attention, something within you that needs healing.

Be Still and Smile

When you find wet towels aging under the bed; when his bedroom floor is covered with empty potato chip bags and pop cans line the windowsill; when she's borrowed your shoes and hasn't put them back or used your new makeup before you had a chance; when he's borrowed your tools to fix his car and now you can't find them—in all these circumstances, being still and breathing helps. Smiling helps. Going for a walk helps. It's okay to take your role as a parent seriously, but take yourself and the situation lightly. You'll build a flourishing alliance with your teen when you look for the humor around you and are willing to smile at the typicalness of it all. With a lighthearted attitude, you'll be able to relax and enjoy each other more.

A thirteen-year-old boy once told me, "Adults talk too much, frown too much; they're too serious; they ought to chill before they get upset." There's common sense in that boy's statement. When was the last time you greeted your teenager with a smile? Is there so much going on that you always look and feel frazzled?

Although life with a teenager can be intolerable at times, one way to get through a troublesome moment is to remind yourself that the more difficult your predicament, the more you need to be still, breathe, and remember that this is your beloved child—is a messy room that important?

Suzanne discovered the be-still-and-smile method of communication by accident: "I had been feeling left out; my fourteen-year-old son, Hank, wasn't talking to me. As soon as he got home, he went straight to his room or out to play basketball. One day when he walked into the kitchen to get something from the refrigerator, I immediately stopped what I was doing, sat down, didn't say a word, and smiled. To my amazement, he sat down too and started telling me about his day. Since he clams up when I ask questions, I didn't ask a question; I nodded, paid attention, and continued smiling. I learned more in that twelve minutes than I had in a month."

Sitting down makes you look available, smiling makes you look friendly, and being still makes you look ready to listen. Remember that teenagers don't like questions from parents—it makes them think they're being cross-examined; they get defensive. But when you're quiet and smiling, they'll sometimes sit down and open up. It's paradoxical that when *you're* not talking, *they're* more apt to jabber. If life with your teenager sometimes doesn't make sense, you'll be ahead when you smile.

Willingly Make Up

There's a popular belief that if you haven't established a loving relationship with your child by the time he or she is a teenager, it's too late. This is only partially true. Your teen wants to have a loving relationship with you and will be open to letting that happen—if you are willing to take responsibility for your part in creating the mess in the first place. Even if your relationship feels hopeless, beyond repair, your teenager secretly hopes for a loving bond. If your relationship is less than desirable, you, the adult, must make the first, second, third, or however many steps it takes to move your relationship in a healthy direction.

Often when I speak, one or two courageous parents will acknowledge that they have not been good parents. They were too strict, too critical, too controlling, not interested in knowing their child, too lenient and disinterested, or emotionally or physically abusive. One mother acknowledged that she was so unhappy with her own life, she didn't want to be bothered with her kids; she felt they were a nuisance. Looking back, she realized she was depressed while they were growing up and now she wants to make things right.

Making up starts with an specific acknowledgment from you of what you've done wrong: "I called you lazy last night and I was wrong," followed by your statement of the truth, "I was in a bad mood and took it out on you." Follow this with your intention to change your behavior: "I don't want to take my frustrations out on you anymore, so when I'm upset I'll go for a walk."

It's never too late to have a relationship with your child; however, you must be willing to apologize for what you've done. Not a blanket apology, but a specific statement about how you've blown it and what you intend to do to change your behavior to make things right. Take an inventory of your past behavior and make amends through your words and actions. If they see you accountable for your actions they will gain this habit too.

Admit when you are baffled. For example, Nancy told her daughter, "I've never been a mother of a teenager before; help me, I'm learning too." When you disagree, say, "I don't agree, but then we won't see eye-to-eye on every issue."

Decide to forgive your teenager when he has hurt you. There is no need to carry around animosity. I've seen parents hold grudges that have lasted a lifetime. We can choose our attitudes, and within in each of us is the ability to turn resentment into forgiveness. There's never any need to throw your teenager out of your heart—not even for a moment.

Respond with an Open Heart

Your relationship with your teenager is a work in progress, so it's bound to be a little crazy at times. You and your teen are so entwined that it's not uncommon for you to react with anger rather than say what you really feel.

Whenever Frank is worried about one of the kids, he talks in an exasperated voice and often he loses his temper rather than say, "I'm concerned about you," in a loving way. After the football game, Dan could see that James, fourteen, felt badly about fumbling the ball. Dan felt badly, too, but instead of reaching out to comfort, he grumbled about the referee. Responding with an open heart means calmly speaking the truth from your deepest self: "I'm sorry you are suffering," or "I'm afraid you are going to get pregnant."

When you respond with an open heart, you let a moment or two of silence pass, so you can see clearly what is in your heart and then reply, if any, is needed. Monitor what you're thinking and feeling before you jump too quickly, because it might not have anything to do with what's troubling your teen.

It's a parent's responsibility to respond in the moment to what's needed, rather than react automatically from past experience or a preconceived notion. This isn't always easy and it requires a great deal of self-awareness. You need to understand your own motivations and learn to get beyond them. As one woman said to me, "I have finally realized that almost all of my anger comes from fear. So when I find myself about to blow up, I ask myself what am I afraid of. I've discovered that so much of my anger at the trivial mistakes my teens make—like forgetting to empty the dishwasher—is my own fear that they will grow up to be irresponsible adults."

One reason kids don't willingly tell parents what is going on is because parents often freak out over what they hear. You make matters worse by getting upset. Even a crisis doesn't have to be turned into a trauma. Every painful situation can be dealt with if you take the time to calmly respond with a open mind and heart. Some parents think that their teenager is deliberately doing things to irritate, harass, or manipulate them. Frankly, sometimes you feel crazed.

Responding with a open heart means you separate the behavior from the child, and your reaction to his behavior from your love for him. It also means frequently saying, "thank you"—every teenager needs to hear a word of gratitude once in a while.

Of course, you can't always be centered and loving; you will blow up, lose it, scream and have a fit, and say things you don't mean. When you do, be gentle with yourself—after all, there's a "crazy teenager" within you too.

Accept Changes Graciously

You know that everything changes, but you're seldom prepared when it comes to your children. When your children are toddlers, change seems gradual; you know you'll have fifteen or more years together. Then suddenly they're teenagers, and the years are flying by. They're all grown up with plans of their own, plans that don't always include you, and you realize that the time together is precious—the years have shortened into months.

As parents, we want to hold tightly to those heart-melting moments when she lost her tooth and you were the Tooth Fairy, or when you bought his baseball glove and taught him to hold a bat. Your babies will always be your babies, but you can't treat them like one anymore. Your girl looks more like a young women now; your son is becoming a man. By the time your son is a teenager, he's had lots of new experiences; if you presume he's thinking as he did when he was ten years old, you're missing a lot. If you're fighting those changes, you're probably getting weary. But if you welcome the changes graciously, you'll be young at heart.

Parents have to change, too—you can't avoid it. Growing up and moving on is a continuous process that your whole family is involved in. Your daughter isn't the same person she was five years ago, and neither are you.

Change brings fresh possibilities, opens windows to surprises ahead. Soon you find that you have more to share. Joella misses helping Cynda pick out a lunch pail each school year and she misses the chalk pictures on the sidewalk; but at the same time, she delights in the excitement of a first dance, and she's proud that Cynda doesn't go along willy-nilly with the crowd. Mary, the mother of a teenage son, misses the family snuggling in bed; now Chuck sits on the couch for a chat. Although she misses the snuggling, she welcomes the adult conversations. She takes pleasure in Chuck's looking out for her: "I'll look in the paper to see if your team won, Mom." Robert misses reading the comics to his son, but he enjoys their Sunday golf game.

It's natural for you to miss the years when they were so cuddly and cute and when you were the center of their world. Sometimes you'll hanker for the past, especially when they're ornery and talking back. As a courageous parent aware of the process of life in which you're involved, you accept the shifts, and turns, shedding your tears while moving forward. Sometimes you'll be glad for the changes, and oftentimes thankful that being a teenager is not a permanent condition.

Add a Splash of Pizzazz to Your Own Life

When your teenager is having all the fun while you're doing all the work, it's time to add a splash of pizzazz to *your* life. If you're overloaded with work, errands, obligations, and chores, if you're easily perturbed and exhausted, if you're accusing your teenager of being irresponsible and lazy—it's time to shift your focus away from your teenager onto yourself. It's time to take stock of your life.

Meg, the mother of two, wanted her very active daughters to enjoy their teen years, so she made sure everything ran smoothly. One day, feeling worn out and resentful, she accused them of taking her for granted. The three of them had a screaming scene in the kitchen, and Meg threatened to take away all their privileges if they didn't "shape up." Two days later, things were back to normal—until the next time when Meg felt taken advantage of.

If you want to avoid the "after-all-I-do-for-you blues," stop blaming your teen because *you're* overworked and overwrought. Blame is counterproductive and doesn't address the underlying issue that you're not taking care of yourself. It's *your* responsibility to see that you get your share of the goodies. You need a dose of juicy living, too, and in order for that to happen, you must give it to yourself.

Parents make many willing sacrifices for their children, and this is as it always will be. But unless you want to be known as a parental martyr, laying guilt trips on your kids so they'll appreciate you, you must learn to balance those sacrifices by making choices that satisfy your soul.

Being raised by a parent who sacrifices her own needs places a burden on a child. On the other hand, it is a joy to be raised by a parent who's living a life that is full and happy. A parent who is content and fulfilled teaches a child to be responsible for his own happiness.

Deanna put all her energy into her children until she realized she was neglecting herself. One day, she announced to her family, "It's time for me to take care of myself a little more." She taught the kids to do the laundry and she took ballet lessons. "I wasn't surprised when the kids came to my recital, she said. "But I *was* surprised when they came in clean clothes!"

Make sure you add some pizzazz to your life by doing whatever makes your heart sing—you will be happier, and your teenager, in turn, will be happier too.

Accentuate What Is Truly Meaningful

As in *The Wizard of* Oz, what we're all searching for is already within us. Just like Dorothy, the Tin Man, and the Cowardly Lion, your teenager imagines she's missing something. She's sure if she could only find the secret ingredient, she'd be popular, pretty, and smart. She looks in magazines and at the movie screen, and she sees fantasy peers who have it all. She tries to compete by finding the right makeup, the perfect nail polish, the latest styles. She wants to be special, fit in, and be happy, so she hangs with the right crowd, dreams of the right boyfriend. In spite of her best efforts, she feels a longing, a hole in her heart and doesn't know why. It's the same with your son. Lost in the world, he hankers for a fast car, aspires to be brave, searches diligently, without knowing why or what for, to find what he yearns for—a way back home, back to his own heart.

Teens, including the troubled ones, need to know that they're already okay just as they are. All teens feel flawed; it's your job to let them know they're grand. Surrounded by a loving family, they have whatever they need to be happy. Happiness is not something to grab or strive for. It comes from within, in quiet moments, swelling up in your own heart. Teach your teenagers to reflect, be silent, to go within. Let them know the answers to life's dilemmas lie within our own hearts—not in the newest CD or in bigger breasts. Emphasize the qualities of the heart, the goodness in one another. Speak to them of the unseen forces in the universe guiding their lives, making miracles.

Although your daughter may not be popular or pretty, and your son may not be the captain of the football team, they have many gifts; they are indeed exquisite. Just as, when loved, the ugly ducking becomes a swan, your teenager will blossom in the light of your gentle care. Don't push them to be what they are not—let them flower naturally, love them totally and unconditionally.

The hope for our future lies in our teenagers, and we need to tell them so. Although we're different, we're also the same. There's dignity in all life, so spread the word. If you're always focused on the problems—looking at the negatives—you'll have no energy to see the sunshine, to smell the rain, to taste vanilla. Show your teenagers how to see what matters—that there's heaven all around us.

By Your Own Example, Teach Them to Pray

Each of us—even teenagers—has a spiritual core. Your beloved teen is a spiritual being with longings and needs of the soul. He needs more than material success, the right clothes, the right friends, the right car, the right education to make it in this world. He'll need a spiritual perspective, a frame of reference to find comfort when the needs of the soul call.

By your example, you can teach your teenager ways to pay attention to these soul needs. Forcing religion down his throat isn't nearly as effective as providing reflective experiences in which he can answer the call of the spirit in his own way.

Begin your day with a little spiritual exercise. I like to wake Amanda to Gregorian chanting on the stereo or to a soulful saxophone. I've talked with her about the miracles in my life so much that she's starting to recognize her own. In fact, we both say it's more fun to live with angels watching over us than to have to do everything ourselves. Our home is our temple; we like to create a reverence in our home with candles, prayer, meditation, flowers, and beauty.

Amanda loves to socialize, but she likes an equal amount of quiet time to center herself.

Fill your life with simple things that make you feel content. The Steins have a family dinner once a week and begin with a blessing for the food on the table and the people sitting around it. They turn off the telephone so they can talk to one another without interruptions. Janelle and her mother walk the dogs each evening. The Martinez family seldom misses church on Sunday mornings.

Prayer is an attitude toward life, the song of a grateful heart. Teach your teenager a respect for all life—rejoice together. Prayer is thankfulness, a heart overflowing with the wonder of it all. Be thankful that your child has grown up with you.

Your relationship with your teen is sacred—there's a sacred trust between you. Regardless of difficulties or misunderstandings, you share a holy bond. Be willing to honor it. In every parent/teen relationship, there's abundant grace to see you through—recognize it, call on it, and show your teenager how to call on it herself. Ask for whatever help you need. Know that this soul is with you by divine will, not just by accident. Honor each member of your family—grandparents, mother, father, teens, children—for your souls are eternally linked.

Treasure Being Together as a Family

Teenagers across the country feel alienated from their families, alienated from adults who give lip service to family values, but have thrown their precious teenage children out of their hearts. There are far too many adults caught up in getting ahead and so focused on their own lives and pressures that they ignore the souls of their teenagers. Teens need more than material advantages; they need more than a college education to succeed. Our teenage children long for the steadfast love of parents and the safety of a home filled with love and communication.

To me, a family home is a place where at the end of the day you retreat, rest, and unwind. In communion with loving family members, you renew your spirit, refresh your soul. Sadly, according to one national survey, most kids think their parents aren't available and they don't expect to have a happy future.

Teenagers have seen adults throw away spouses, parents, and siblings who displeased them, so it's no wonder that teens worry that they don't belong. Far too many teens feel shut out, thrown out, or shoved aside by adults who don't want to be bothered. Drug abuse, alcoholism, promiscuity, violence, depression, and suicide are all symptoms of broken hearts and broken families that don't know how to connect.

Teens want to be part of a family, especially one that's glad they're a member, glad they showed up, glad to have them around—and show it. When your daughter comes home from a hard day at school and you're glad to see her, whether or not she shows it, she's no doubt glad you noticed. If your son doesn't have positive feelings of belonging to his family, he'll turn even more to friends; he'll look somewhere else.

Give your children a sense of how much they're needed in your family, that you're a team, that you pull together. Let them know that you are committed to them—that the family bond will never be broken. Create a family motto. Amanda and I say, "We're rich—rich in love." Teens can benefit from an extended family of grandparents, aunts, uncles, and cousins. Make an effort to keep in touch or reconnect with family for your children's sake. The Smiths seldom see their relatives because they live so far away, so they've purposely created a family of close friends and neighbors. Knowing they have this adopted family to have fun with, to celebrate with, or to turn to in an emergency, is very reassuring.

It's the unconditional love within that family that will soothe what ails you.

Do the Best You Can

There will be times when nothing works, when nothing you do or say will make things better. No matter what parenting skills you employ, no matter how loving, kind, fair, understanding, courteous, or brilliant you are, there will be painful times when your daughter won't cooperate, when she'll call you names. There will be times when your son will go behind your back and disobey you. There will be times when nothing makes it right—times when they don't like you and you don't like them!

When everything you do is a source of irritation for her, when he's quarrelsome, disrespectful, and downright belligerent, do you wonder where you've failed? Do you wish you could start over, do it better? Do you strive to have a good relationship, yet secretly yearn for the peace and quiet when he moves out?

You are not alone. Parents feel guilty about a lot of things. We worry that we have inflicted our own insecurities and inadequacies on our children. We fear they've inherited our legacy of pain. We wonder if we've taught them what they need to know to succeed. We doubt ourselves and are sure we've messed up as parents by not doing it "right." We're hard on ourselves. We're afraid we're bad parents. We know we worry too much about their setbacks and we take on too much responsibility for their future—but we can't help it. After all, we're parents and we want the best for them.

When things go wrong, we put on the pressure. We're aware of our own imperfections, so we try to instill perfection in our kids. As one father told me, "I do it for his own good." He was afraid that if he didn't correct his son Eli, that Eli would miss out on opportunities. "He has so much potential. I don't want him to mess up like I did."

Perfection is such a bitter pill. It makes you tense and doesn't cure a thing. It's okay to be "good enough." Just because your child has a problem doesn't automatically mean you've messed up. Say to yourself: I'm doing the best I can with what I know. Then be gentle with yourself. Al and Sue, the parents of twin teenage boys, told me, "Our boys are enthusiastic about life—and that's good enough."

Ask for Input
About the Toughies

There are a multitude of tough issues surrounding teenagers—curfews, dating, driving, money, chores, homework, styles, friends, drinking. Sometimes you can't possibly fathom what to do. Teens have a wide array of dilemmas to cope with, so don't despair if you can't come up with all the answers on your own. You need input from your teenager, from friends, and from advisers. Gather information and get feedback. You have many sources to turn to, including your teenager, other parents, parenting classes, and support groups. Lynne said, "When I'm upset or worried, I handle things much better when I talk it over with other parents first." Many other parents have successfully traversed this territory. They may have workable suggestions you never dreamed of.

Open and honest communication is the key. Ask your teenagers what they think about the tough issues: the social scene, dating, curfew, and money. Ask them, "What do *you* think?" They'll cooperate more readily when they've participated in solving the matter. Mark says, "When Hank asks to go to parties, I try to say yes as much as possible. I ask myself if there is any good reason why he can't go?

Then I ask Hank the same question. If we can't think of any good reasons why he shouldn't go, I tell him to have a good time. If we do think of a reason why he shouldn't go, together we try to find a way to deal with the problem so that he *can* go."

When you encourage your teenager's involvement in handling the tough issues, there will be less friction between you—and a lot more understanding. The Lopes family talked about money and allowances with their kids. Because seventeen-year-old Theresa had a part-time job and earned spending money, she suggested forfeiting her allowance; her parents agreed to help out with unexpected or large expenses. Juan, thirteen, wanted a regular allowance, payable on Fridays, so he could buy comic books. Other families find different solutions.

Elizabeth and her twins don't like allowances, so she gives them spending money as it's needed or when they ask. "They never abuse the privilege. When they ask for something I can't afford, I explain why I'm saying no. They usually understand. They may pout sometimes, but they don't give me a hard time."

When tough questions pop up—and they always do—you'll need help. A father in a parenting class expressed it best: "Being a parent of a teenager is filled with never-ending challenges for which I'm not entirely suited, so I think of myself as a consultant and a researcher, trying to find the answers—some I found, some I'm still searching for."

Encourage Role Models

For every teenager who has made her dreams come true, someone has shown her the way. *Mentoring* is believing in another person and offering counsel as to how she can fulfill her dreams. A mentor gives a perspective that others may have overlooked and believes in you even when you have lost belief in yourself. All teenagers, no matter how good their parents are, need mentors—wise adults, grandparents, counselors, and teachers who are willing to go out of their way, stand alongside them, and point the way. Our job as parents is to encourage such adult role models and not be jealous if our kids find them.

Seth wanted a part-time job, but because of school and home obligations could work only occasional, irregular hours. A cynic told him that no one would hire a teenager with demands. His neighbor encouraged him to go for his ideal job, outlined the steps, then cheered him on. Seth filled out twelve job applications, and attached recommendations as well as a letter explaining what he was looking for and why. Eleven places turned him down cold; he was discouraged, but his mentor kept the faith. Eventually, one owner of a làtte stand, impressed by Seth's initiative, changed his policy and hired and trained him to work on call.

Adults have great opportunities to affect the attitudes and behavior of teenagers. We have the power to set the tone, teach respect, and instill enthusiasm. If we do nothing, we leave our teenagers to the mercy of cynics, con artists, and opportunists who use kids to their own advantage. Teens thrive on practical experience, realistic how-to's, and large doses of optimism. A teenager led by a positive role model rises to the occasion.

As parents, we need to acknowledge the special teachers in our children's lives who are doing outstanding jobs. It's okay to complain when something is wrong; however, it's equally important to praise and show gratitude for the outstanding, dedicated work they are doing on our children's behalf. Write a letter today to the teacher, coach, or mentor, acknowledging them for going the extra mile.

Become a Mentor

There are wide discrepancies in the teenage experience. Whereas some teenagers have the protection of a loving family and a stable home, far too many others cope daily with poverty, violence, chaos, and abuse. Although their lifestyles may be diverse, their needs are not.

Teenagers need not only a dose of compassion and understanding for their plight, but also responsible, trustworthy adults willing to give a helping hand, willing to do whatever it takes to ensure that our communities, our country, our world is focused on the needs of our children and adolescents. What better goal could there be? Just because they have reached their teens and in many ways are highly competent, that doesn't mean we can leave them to their own resources and look the other way.

Boys and girls both need a masculine presence in their lives. If you are a man, look around and you'll find a boy or girl in your vicinity who is without a dad. Rich took his two sons to the father/son banquet and included one friend who otherwise would not have gone. Rod, the father of two, is always helping out his daughter's friends. He helped Art buy a computer, he oversees Amanda's car, and he teaches the kids in the neighborhood how to fix their bikes.

There are many ways to help out, and in doing so, you teach teens the value of pulling together, the joy of neighborly kindness. When you extend a helping hand to a teen, you build a bridge to a young person who might otherwise feel left out and bitter. By your example, you help them develop identity and pride, as well as a sense of belonging to a community. A teen who knows that someone cares enough to show it by their actions keeps moving in a positive direction, and that has a ripple effect that touches all our lives.

There are many ways you can become a mentor for a teen. Philip became a Big Brother for a local agency. Victoria became a foster grandparent to a teenage girl. Stuart talks to teens who hang around his garage, and he shows them how to hold a wrench and hammer. Ginger makes sure the cookie jar is always full and invites her daughter's friends to help themselves. She has made her home a warm place for teens to visit.

Don't give up—teens need you.

Expand Your Vision
for Our Children

We hope for a better world for our children, yet we wonder if it's possible. We want peace, yet things are so unsettled. As the mothers and fathers of the world, we must hold steady in our determination to give our teenagers what they so deserve. By giving our time, our love, our unending support, our abiding faith, our teenagers can have a fulfilling life.

Mothers and fathers must take action to create safe communities for all teenagers. Teens need places to go, to hang out, to have fun, to learn. They need safe streets and clean air. Teens worry about their future, they wonder about their opportunities, and to some it seems like life is a dead-end. One thirteen year old told me, "I don't think I'll live very long."

What kind of a world do we want for our teenagers? What are you willing to do until every teenager is cared for, until every teenager has opportunities? Without a strong vision for our teenagers, they will not make it. If all mothers and fathers give up on teenagers, we'll all be in a sorry state. As one mother eloquently said, "With faith in myself, my fellow man, and with God's love guiding me, I'll keep fighting for our teenagers."

Make a commitment to our children to make your community a better place, and tell one person what you plan to do. Ask others what they're doing. If your community is doing all right, reach out to another that's not so fortunate. It's not enough to say, "I'm afraid for our teenagers." You must be willing to do something—beginning right now!

Spirit

Life with your teenager is full of surprises, full of absurdity, full of the ridiculous. If you are serious, you will miss it all. Teens need assurance through words and actions of your everlasting love, and although they might behave with indifference, your expressions of affection do matter.

Try the Playful Approach

With a teenager at home, you'll seldom have a dull moment—there's always something going on: "Dad, it's just a little dent." "But Mom, it's *my* hair!" "Yes, everyone is sleeping over—what's wrong with *that*?" You'll probably panic more than once—especially when they tell you about their latest adventure or insist on trying the newest fad. It's natural for you to worry; after all, you want to protect them the best you can. But if you learn to use a playful approach, instead of freaking out at all the mood swings and seemingly crackpot ideas, you and your family will be energized and excited, hassles will resolve more quickly, and tensions will dissolve with less antagonism.

The years from thirteen through nineteen are known for drama and intensity of feeling, but you won't get so frazzled by the ups and downs of your teenager's daily life when you take the playful approach. A comedian knows that timing is important for delivering a punch line, the same is true for you and your teenager. With careful timing, a playful word can turn a potential confrontation into willing cooperation. When you learn how, where, and when to be playful, you'll enjoy each other more while getting your point across.

Fourteen-year-old Mark was disagreeing with every word his mother said. "I wouldn't call the sky blue," he said. "It's actually more grayish." "Just because I eat pizza, it doesn't mean I like it." "Don't assume I want to talk with you just because I'm listening." After a couple of days of this dead-end conversation, his mom was losing her patience and said good-naturedly, "I know your job as a teenager is to argue with every word I say, but tonight I'm worn out, so will you take a vacation from your job? You can start again tomorrow." He chuckled and was pleasant the entire evening.

What is the playful approach? It's finding a way to make your point while letting your teen save face. The playful approach lets everyone relax so that the heat of the moment doesn't turn into a bonfire. It means knowing when to lighten up. Teenagers know when they're pushing the limits of your patience, but sometimes they can't stop. When you freak out, embarrass, ridicule, or threaten, you back them into a corner, and so they defend their position even harder.

A playful observation from you can turn a confrontation around. Greg got a speeding ticket and was defensive when his dad, Allen, wanted to talk about it. Allen started to yell, then stopped, and with a lilt in his voice said, "I know you don't need me to advise you, but if I don't act like a parent, I think I'm not doing my job, so bear with me while I lecture." Greg nodded, understood, and listened. When they came to a resolution, Greg asked, "Feel better now, Dad?"

Use the playful approach with your teenagers, and they might learn to use it with you.

Have Exciting Conversations

If the only conversations you're having with your teenagers are filled with questions, reprimands, or advice, they probably won't talk with you much. Because teenagers thrive on excitement and avoid parental input and opinions, I recommend that you use the gift of gab to develop an exciting, informative dialogue. It's a way to discover what they're thinking and feeling, to find out what is happening, and to be actively involved.

When you have exciting conversations, your teen won't be as defensive, so you can slip in your philosophy without him even knowing it. Through exciting conversations, you can influence him without scrutinizing his every move.

An exciting conversation is made up of four phases: the telling of the story or events, careful listening to the story, timing your response, and opening the door for continued dialogue.

To have an exciting conversation, you must become an expert at listening. If he never shares with you what's on his mind, he's probably sharing with someone who really listens. If you assume that you already know what your teenager is saying, you'll tend to jump in with advice so quickly he will shut down when you're in the room.

I have discovered that many parents don't listen completely. In fact, most parents can't listen for one full minute without interrupting, offering a piece of advice, or trying to fix the problem. To improve your listening, try this exercise: Set a timer for one minute and don't say a word. Practice this alone until you've learned to mentally calculate a "listening minute." The next time your teen talks, you'll be prepared to respond with the listening minute before you utter one word.

The listening minute is followed by a listening response: "I think that's a great idea." "What happened?" "I'm wondering what you think about . . ." "That happened to me too." You can also use minuscule questions to invite continued dialogue: "Mmm?" "Oh?" "What did you do next?" "Have you thought about . . .?" "Really?"

Sally listened so well that her fourteen-year-old son, Eric, confessed to sneaking into the movies. "I listened for about two minutes and then said, 'Really?' After he shared more, instead of delivering a lecture, Sally gave a response that showed she was really listening: "I did the same thing when I was seventeen." This led to a twenty-minute discussion about peer pressure and knowing right from wrong.

No matter how great a conversationalist you become, your teenager will never talk your ear off—but your friends, neighbors, and relatives might, so use your new skills discreetly!

Consider Their Point of View

Teens see things with a fresh perspective, and if you listen with an open heart, they'll feel safe enough to share their point of view. Teenagers tell the truth with such alarming candor that you'll be startled and delighted when they let you in on what they observe. Here are some things teens have told me. Wouldn't you agree that their frankness is amazing?

Brian, thirteen: "I've never seen an entire family have fun together at the same time. It works best when it's just me and Mom, or me and Dad, or me and my brother. When we're all together, there's always something to fight about, or someone's mad, or we all can't agree. We even fight on Christmas morning. Someone's always telling you when you can open your presents and where to put the paper. I guess the most fun we have is when we let the cats in and watch them play with the paper."

Jolee, fifteen: "I think adults are afraid of teenagers, because we're still free and they're not."

Over and over, teens tell me: "I wish my parents would listen more" . . . "My parents are too suspicious" . . . "I wish my parents would consider what I want—how I want to live my life." When your teenager says you're overreacting, perhaps it's time to consider her point of view.

Lindy said, "My mom gets upset when I tell her stuff, but my dad listens to my side of the story."

Listening to their point of view, their side of the story, means you'll stop long enough to reflect on what they're saying. To consider your teenager's point of view, you need to adopt the attitude: *You might be right; I'd like to think that over*, or *I see what you mean; I never looked at it that way*. It's music to their ears when you say, "I've been thinking about what you said . . ."

Finding out what they're thinking and considering their point of view is different from interrogating them. Teens don't like pointed questions. If you're are too specific, they clam up. Don't act like a detective trying to uncover all the details and facts. Teens don't respond well to: "Where did you go?" "What did you do?" "Did you get all your homework done?" "Have you practiced your piano?" "What are you doing Saturday night?" "Who's going to be there?" As Amanda told me, "Generic questions only, Mom."

Share Your Perspective

You can have influence over your teenager's life if you are willing to thoughtfully share your perspective. Sharing is gently letting him in on what you are thinking without insisting that he see it your way. It's an open-minded examination of differing points of view, looking at all the options, considering all the choices. Rules, discipline, punishment, and control breed hostility in a teenager, for when she feels forced to do it your way, she'll dig in her heels and refuse to budge. On the other hand, mindfully sharing your slant on what's going on might sway her in your direction.

Tim never talked with his son; mostly, he barked orders or criticized with comments like: "Don't you know any better?" "I'm doing this for your own good." "If all your friends jumped off a bridge, would you?" "How could you be so stupid?" Secretly, fifteen-year-old Sam felt ashamed. He wondered why his father never explained things. He wished for a dad who was reasonable.

Most teenagers resent being talked down to. In fact, the more your child loves you, the more he will feel insulted by berating, chastising, scolding, or lecturing. Talking down to your daughter breaks her heart, undermines her confidence, confuses the issues, and increases her inner turmoil—and then she never hears a word. Instead of demanding that she listen or do it your way, as a reasonable parent you'll gingerly share your outlook so you'll be able to give valuable input without causing hard feelings.

Martha talked a lot when her children were around. She commented on the latest happenings in the neighborhood; she knew the teachers at the high school, and let her kids know if she disagreed with a teacher's perspective. She had opinions on politics and was active in her church. She told her children what she thought of teen pregnancy, and she wouldn't tolerate disrespectful behavior. She admitted when she wasn't sure.

Vocalize your values and standards. One study showed that kids who hear their parents talking about values make better choices themselves. Let them know your opinions. Give your perspective. Share your philosophy of life and how you arrived at it. Have conversations with other adults and let them listen in.

Aletha and Art, the parents of three teenagers, noticed that whenever they invited friends over and had heated conversations about politics, money, movies, religion, and the like, the kids liked to hang around, listen in, and contribute. By sharing your point of view in an open-minded way, you create a friendly atmosphere that draws your teen a little closer. Then when something pops up that needs to be talked over, the favorable climate you've created will ease your discussion in a positive way.

Provide Adventures

Teenagers are naturally lively and vivacious, and you know that with such energetic spirit in your house, you won't be bored for long. They are full of curiosity—eager to try new things, brimming with fervor, willing to take risks, and searching for adventure. They like excitement and intrigue—as a way of mastering life, of learning more about themselves, and of discovering their potential. They want to take on the world and branch out beyond the family. With such vibrant energy, they want to learn it all, see it all, experience it all. As sixteen-year-old Trisha said, "I don't want to miss a thing."

When you recognize your teen's urge to explore as a sign of growing up, you'll see it in a positive light. That thirst for experiencing life on his own is the instinctual drive that propels him into adulthood. Without it, he would never leave home; he would be a child forever.

Margee was worried because her fifteen-year-old-son, Jerome, spent most of the weekends watching TV or going fishing alone. As the summer approached, she hoped that he would show some interest in getting a job or at the very least keep his room clean and do his share of the chores, but he lacked motivation and refused to cooperate. Jerome admitted that he was bored. "My parents won't let me go fishing out of state with my friend's family, and they won't let me work on the park clean-up crew. They don't want me to be away from home; they don't want me to grow up." The damper Jerome's parents put on his adventurous spirit was causing him to passively resist doing anything.

Adventures don't have to be dangerous to excite teens. They are always eager to learn, especially if it's something they love. Ask your teenager what she likes to do for fun that takes one minute, five minutes, or five hours. Then start incorporating fun and excitement into each day. Mini-adventures, such as having a picnic dinner at the park, can add spice to life and give you quality time together as well.

Teens can use your input to find positive adventures they may not have considered. At thirteen, David learned to read the bus schedule, and at fifteen it's his main mode of transportation. When Emma, thirteen, proclaimed that she was bored, her parents suggested a range of options: summer camp, a plane ride alone to visit grandparents, horseback-riding lessons. Max, fourteen, loved the outdoors, so the entire family took up kayaking. Alice could see that her daughter wasn't using her natural artistic talent, so in order to give her encouragement and exposure to the artistic world, they took a watercolor class together.

Your teenager will have adventures—that is a given. Some you will approve of, others will keep you awake at night. But what can you do? When she was a child, you could support her thirst for adventure by something as simple as a change in routine; now that she is a teenager, it's more complicated. I don't know any parents who have found the answer except to pray that they are safe.

Include Lots of Friends

Once your child starts the seventh grade, you'll have to move over and make room for friends. You won't be the center of his social life any longer. He'll be making new acquaintances and discovering what other people are like. Don't take it personally if your daughter won't go shopping with you anymore; it doesn't mean she is rejecting you. "My mom thinks I don't like her anymore, just because I'd rather be with my friends." Friendships take effort and energy—and your daughter is focusing on maintaining her friendships now.

Thirteen-year-old Heidi was a social butterfly. She told her mom, "I want to have everyone in my class over for dinner." Her mother, Allison, was leery at first, and at times it was a hassle, but she made the commitment and followed through. One by one, she invited her classmates until all thirty-two, including the teacher, had been entertained. They called the evenings "friendship dinners," and the positive feedback outweighed the extra work. Heidi helped with the dinner and dishes, and Allison got acquainted with the other parents. Though your child may not be as gregarious as Heidi, you'll reap clear rewards when you don't stand in the way of your teenager making friends.

Girls make friends by talking with one another—gabbing, gossiping, sharing secrets, making idle chatter, laughing. That's the main reason the phone is so important to them. Your daughter will want to have slumber parties so she can talk, talk, talk all night.

Boys make friends by doing something together, which is why team sports and group activities attract their interest. If your son isn't interested in sports, help him find a group activity—perhaps a computer club, the debate team, or the band. To make friends, your son needs at least one weekly activity where he can do something with boys his own age.

Remember that your teenager wants to be popular and appreciated as an individual. Refrain from criticizing your child's choice of friends, or you'll likely make things worse. Richard was appalled when sixteen-year-old Seth brought home two boys with shaved heads and rings in their noses, but he held his tongue. In less than two months, Seth joined the wrestling team with one of the boys; the other one drifted away. Given the chance, your teenager can make good choices in friends. Friendships change and evolve—some last, others don't.

Every parent of a teen knows that if you want to see your teenager once in a while—if you want them hanging around your house, if you want them to go to the movies with you or out to dinner, if you want them with you on a vacation—you need to invite their friends along. It's the "more the merrier" stage of life.

Make Room for the Blues

Teenagers frequently feel gloomy, dejected, depressed, and disheartened. Like us, they get down in the dumps. Although they might not talk with you about it, you can see it by the look on his face, the sadness in her eyes, his temperamental disposition, or her moody silence. If you look only at the surface, you might not understand the significance of these times.

Everyone's had the blues. They sometimes come for no identifiable reason—out of nowhere it hits you like a wave, and you're feeling sad but you're not sure why. It's the same with teenagers; they're sensitive human beings affected by what's going on around them. Not only are they influenced by the rush of hormones, they're bombarded daily from all sides with messages that tug at their tender souls.

As they emerge from childhood and blossom into teenagers, they become more attuned to the world at large. Unfortunately, this is not always a pretty picture. They start to comprehend the enormity of the world and understand that life can be unfair. They're faced with the realities of crime, misfortune, atrocities, and evil. The existential questions pop up, and they ask themselves: *Who am I? Where am I going, and why?* These questions spark a spiritual quest, and they wonder: *How can I make a difference? How can I impact the world?* It's a profound time of inner searching, and sometimes they feel hopeless, helpless, and distraught.

Puberty not only brings bodily changes, it also requires emotional and psychological adjustments. And boys and girls alike have apprehensions and anxieties about the continuous physical changes they are undergoing.

When the blues come, the best thing you can do for teenagers is to kindly treat them with compassion—offer a hug, a tender look, a pat on the shoulder. These are things you cannot fix. You can't make the feelings go away with a pep talk, advice, or reassurance. It's through your gentle actions and loving-kindness that you let them know you walk with them in spirit, that you hold them in the light.

Just one person's love can make a difference. "When I got sad, my parents got mad, so I'd go talk to my grandma," said Angie. "She never asked questions like my parents did, but she always held my hand."

"When my best friend moved out of state, I was so upset I couldn't talk. My mom took me to the beach, and I sat on a log and cried. She said she was sorry I felt so lonely and asked if she could give me a hug."

We all get the blues. It's okay to be down for a day or two, or even a week, but if the blues last longer and are affecting sleep, appetite, or schoolwork, be sure to seek the advice of a professional.

Show Wholehearted Interest Without Taking Over

I asked a group of high-school students what advice they would give to parents. Here's what they had to say:

• Really support your kids. Show up at the activities they participate in and show enthusiasm. You can really tell which kids get support from their parents and which ones don't. It makes a big difference.

• A teenager feels isolated and detached, and flounders around lonely and in despair when his parents are not interested in what he's doing.

• The parents who show up at activities get acquainted with the other kids and parents. When you know each other, your school becomes a community and helps everyone feel safe.

• A teenager wants her parents to share and be onlookers, not run the show and take over. Learn about their music, the hair styles, the slang—but don't adopt them for yourself. Learn about their culture without becoming a part of it. Your teenager wants you to behave like a grownup. In other words, if you're a parent, don't behave or dress like a teenager.

• Susie and Aimee didn't mind teaching their single mothers the slang for meeting guys, but they definitely didn't want their single mothers adopting their style.

• It's a courteous gesture to ask permission before you get involved. Don't sign up to be his soccer coach unless your son has agreed beforehand, and don't volunteer to help in her computer lab unless she's given you the go-ahead.

• Be sensitive to the dividing line between enthusiastically supporting them and taking over. When they know they're in charge of the boundaries, they will let you come closer.

Here is a case in point: Cindy asked Derek, "Do you want me to come to your baseball games?"

"You can come to the home games, but not the out-of-town games," he replied.

"Do you mind if I volunteer to help at the games?

"As long as it's in the concession stand. I don't want you keeping score."

Although she didn't understand his reasoning, Cindy respected Derek's wishes: "By keeping my distance, he's let me become even more involved. Last week, he asked me to drive to his last out-of-town game."

Try asking your own kids: "Do you want me to come?" "I'd like to volunteer—what job should I do?" "What advice do you have for me?"

If you've never asked such questions before, your teen will probably be suspicious and might not answer right away. But if you're sincere and ready to heed her advice, you can have lots of fun being involved without taking over. Your place is on the sidelines, cheering her on, not sharing the spotlight.

Find New Ways to Be Together

To raise a teen and enjoy it you need chutzpah, imagination, daring, and a dose of audacity. You also need to become proficient at adding sprinkles of togetherness throughout your week—capturing spontaneous moments, flashes of time where everyday routine bursts into a heartfelt connection.

Mike told me that some of the best moments with his two teenage sons came when he said, "I'm going on an errand, come with me," and they ended up at a dog show or browsing through a used-car lot. One day, he asked his sons to help build some bookshelves. The boys not only learned to use the tools, they learned to work together. It was so much fun that they sawed and hammered each Saturday until they'd lined two closets with shelves.

Jolene likes to plan surprises for her thirteen and fifteen year olds. "My kids like surprises, and it tickles them when I do something out of the ordinary." On the spur of the moment, Jolene has delivered breakfast in bed, put bubbles in their bathwater, served banana splits for dinner, and taught them the joy of shopping at garage sales.

One father drives two hours each Sunday to visit his twins and browse their favorite used-book store. The Madisons said about their son Parker: "When he was about thirteen, he still liked going places with our family. At fourteen, he started resisting. By fifteen, he just wasn't interested anymore. We used to enjoy car trips, but by sixteen he didn't want to go, and forcing him didn't work. Finally, we accepted that if we wanted to be together as a family, we'd have to figure out a new way."

It's a fact that teens don't want to be with parents in the same way or as much as when they were younger. The activities you once enjoyed, such as family vacations, afternoons at the beach, or going out to dinner, might still appeal to you, but chances are you'll have to find a new angle to entice your teenager to come along.

You can put a new spin on togetherness by taking a class together—anything from cooking to photography. Or do something physical such as roller-blading, jogging, karate, or yoga. Join a gym or go swimming. Teens like excitement, so keeps things lively. Whether it's a week-long vacation or an half-day outing, do something you've never done before.

And don't forget to spice up your home life by doing the unexpected—put on the music and invite them to dance. And when they look dumbfounded, ignore it, and keep on dancing.

Celebrate the Milestones

In Bali, the rite of passage from childhood to adulthood is a tooth-filing ceremony. The community watches as each teenager has his front teeth filed perfectly straight. Everyone looks forward to the event: It's a big celebration, the relatives come dressed in their finery, and the food is lavish. It's a turning point because the teenager is honored as he or she moves into the adult world.

In our culture, turning points include getting a driver's license and going to the prom. The prom is not just a high-school dance; it's a symbol of growing up—a marker of time—where your son acts like an adult by dressing in a tuxedo, taking a girl to dinner, paying the bill, driving the car, and staying out late.

Recognizing these passages as special events is rewarding and fun for the whole family. It brings you together and perpetuates tradition. When Sally started junior high, her parents marked the day by writing a silly poem and sticking it in her notebook. When Kelly got her braces off, the Hollands called Grandma and bragged about her looks.

It's a long-standing tradition in the Becker family to throw a "sweet sixteen" party for each child. The entire clan comes to honor the person turning sixteen; it's a friendly roast of sorts, with family members sharing memories and funny stories about the honoree. (And by the way, sixteen really *is* a "sweet" time. Sixteen year olds are more settled, more understanding, and less volatile then when they were from thirteen to fifteen, and they're friendly and eager to communicate.)

Passing on family history is important when you find a way to do it without boring your kids to death. Denise recognized her two teenagers and seven of her teenage nephews and nieces by giving them each an album of family pictures and favorite stories and memories. Tina makes cookbooks with family recipes and stories about each dish—including the special peanut-butter pie that Grandpa likes—and gives them as graduation presents.

Don't forget to praise the little events too. Flowers for auditioning for the school play, a CD for running for office, a special dinner for getting the term paper done on time and surviving finals. The Shimadas bring out the ice-cream cake each time their kids put out a lot of effort: "Regardless of the outcome, we celebrate for trying."

Don't forget to celebrate *you* too. Tell them, "My birthday's right around the corner." "Father's Day is Sunday; let's go to the movies." If they forget, it's okay; cheerfully remind them!

Carry on Family Traditions

Although you might get the impression from your teenager's lackadaisical attitude that he isn't interested in your family traditions anymore, don't let his aloofness fool you. His connection to the family is strengthened by family rituals and celebrations. Just because he might act disinterested, this is definitely not the time to stop celebrating meaningful events. It's during these occasions that teenagers learn about their family and make memories. Wrapped in this sense of continuity, they feel safe in their connection with you.

From the time Scott was one year old, Patricia made a big deal of birthdays by baking him a special cake. The year he turned sixteen, she thought he would be embarrassed by a homemade cake, so she bought one from a bakery. Scott was indignant when she served the cake, and said, "Where's my funny-shaped birthday cake?" She took the hint, and the very next day served him a green cake in the shape of a jeep—his favorite car. She could tell he was pleased when he said, "This is the best one yet!", and asked, "What are you doing next year?"

Family traditions are opportunities to come together, reminding us that we are part of a special family unit—our own clan, our gang. When you take time out from your hectic life to honor each other, you reinforce the message: *We're glad to be a family.*

Family traditions observed out of obligation don't do much for unity, so avoid getting locked in to the same old methods—be flexible. When your kids have lost their enthusiasm for participating, test a new angle, try a new twist.

The O'Neals took pride in the photo greeting they sent each holiday, so they were puzzled when fourteen-year-old Liza balked at being included. The struggle was on: the parents insisting she participate as always; Liza making a fuss, alleging that the picture was "stupid." When nothing would sway Liza, their seventeen year old suggested a photo shoot in the park. Suddenly, Liza acquiesced, and instead of a formal family portrait in a studio, the O'Neals were photographed relaxed on the swings; the next year they were climbing a tree. A new slant on an old tradition began.

You'll get more cooperation from everyone if you refresh your old traditions when necessary. Ask for input: "How shall we celebrate Hanukkah this year? Is turkey for Thanksgiving important?" A new angle can liven things up. For example, the Laings wanted the same turkey dinner but not the same formal dining, so they included the neighbors and friends and served the meal buffet style. With more people, Thanksgiving was more lively—and less work. With meaningful yet flexible traditions, your adult children will be more inclined to pass on fond memories to your grandchildren. Now that's cause for celebration!

Bring on the Blaring Music

Teens like music—loud, blaring music! I'm sure that as a teen you did, too—but that's where the similarity ends and the generation gap begins. No matter your age, you know you are a parent of a teenager when the popular music starts sounding like scrambled words and screeching. In the '50s, parents were shocked at Elvis' rotating hips. The Beatles kicked off a clash between teens who wanted long hair and parents who objected. I remember my grandmother complaining that my choice in music as a teen hurt her ears, and when I heard myself voicing the same complaint over Amanda's blaring stereo, I knew I was suddenly part of the older generation.

Nowadays kids not only listen to music, they watch it on videos. Soon after he subscribed to cable, Rob discovered that his fourteen-year-old son, Andy, was fascinated by music videos; and, after watching for a while, Rob understood the appeal, yet was concerned about the violence and sexual innuendo. He felt awkward, but decided to say something to Andy: "Hey, those are pretty sexy numbers you're watching." Andy replied, "Yep, some of them are really gross." After a couple of weeks, Andy wasn't watching music videos anymore, and Rob asked him why. Andy said, "They're all the same—it's boring."

Music you don't understand is here to stay, so you might want to think about how you will handle it. Do what seems right for you. For example, although they know their two teenagers will see music videos, the Kramers told me, "We've decided not to bring it into our home. The kids can listen, but it's too much to watch."

Teens like the music loud and might play it twenty-four hours a day if you weren't around. Margaret, the mother of twenty-year-old Jeff, who is now living in an apartment with friends, told me that she used to yell, "Turn that music down!" but now she misses coming up the driveway to the blaring music, she misses the floors and walls shaking, and she misses him.

Teens love music, and one study found that doing homework to Mozart helped with concentration. There's even a Seattle school that plays Mozart for math class and study hall. Jeremy and his fourteen-year-old buddies have started a rock band and practice in the garage. "The music sounds awful," his parents admit, "but we're happy that we know where to find him." Mike shared his love of Bach and the Grateful Dead with his daughter, Shannon, who wrote a term paper about parents and music.

Blaring music is here to stay, so the issue is one of cooperation, of how you handle it. Some parents buy headphones for the kids, others let it blare when they aren't around. Some folks let the kids listen so long as they turn it down when asked. It's up to you and your kids to work it out.

Allow for Lots of Privacy

Teenagers need lots of privacy! In order to evolve as individuals, they need both physical and emotional distance from you. This can be frustrating if you don't understand the significance.

Some parents wonder what in the world is going on behind those closed doors. As Lynne, the mother of a fifteen-year-old son, asked, "What is he doing in his bedroom all weekend? Shouldn't he be with the family?" Even though parents know that they shouldn't snoop or barge in without knocking, sometimes the urge to know what's going on takes over.

Behind those closed doors, teens are listening to music, talking on the phone, staring into space, reading books or magazines, getting to know their bodies, looking in the mirror, daydreaming, writing in a diary.

Writing in a diary is a conversation with oneself, a way of considering many feelings and ideas. It's one way teens can work things out, and is a good problem-solving device. It's a private, getting-to-know-yourself exercise. Don't snoop there either!

Amy shared with a parenting group what she learned when she unlocked fourteen-year-old Allison's desk drawer and read her diary. "I don't know why I did it. I guess I thought I had the right—after all, I knew her so well. I'd changed her diapers, we shared so much, been so close, I didn't like her having secrets. I read almost the entire diary, page after page filled with her private thoughts and feelings. Allison's description of her first kiss, her feelings toward boys, her worries, her victories. When I read what she had written about me, 'Sometimes I'm rude to my mom. I don't mean to be, but I can't help myself,' I realized I had no business snooping.

"I don't know what I was looking for—nothing really surprised me. It was all very innocent, normal, natural. I felt ashamed. I was invading my daughter's privacy and I knew I had violated an unspoken, sacred trust. I carefully put things back, and she never knew—but I do. I try to make it up to her now, by treating her with the dignity she deserves."

Although it might be somewhat traumatic and require adjustment on your part, it's natural for your teenager to spend considerable time alone in his bedroom. He has secrets and private thoughts. He'll keep things from you that he eagerly shares with friends. If you ask too many questions, you're likely to hear, "That's none of your business"—and he's right! That means no snooping, meddling, listening in. You'll have to mind your own business—nosiness is definitely out.

Carefully Avoid
Embarrassing Them

It seems to be a law of the teenage years that the minute they hit puberty, you do something to embarrass them. Perhaps it's because all their body changes give them heightened self-consciousness. You can tell when you've embarrassed them by the way they roll their eyes and sigh. Sometimes they give you instructions and say clearly, "Mom, don't do that!" Or they give you a look that says, *You're humiliating me!* When you get a direct message, it's a good idea to take into account their feelings and attempt to figure out what they're communicating before you proceed. They're self-conscious enough without your adding to it.

"Behaving themselves" in public can be puzzling for parents, however. You don't mean to embarrass your kids; in fact, you go out of your way to behave according to the unwritten rules of parental protocol. You try to say the right thing, wear acceptable clothes, stand in the background, let your kid run the show. Even with all your consideration, there are times when you think you're behaving appropriately and make what you think is a reasonable comment, and immediately they're mortified!

I asked teenagers: "What do your parents do that embarrasses you?" Here's a partial list of what they said: Talk loudly in public, ask weird questions to strangers, get impatient with waiters or sales clerks, ask my friends questions about their parents, complain about the food when we go out to dinner, get drunk, and make a big deal about nothing.

One rule of thumb is: What's okay in private is not okay in public. Ellen says: "My son and I have an unspoken understanding—I won't fuss over him in public. I let him take the lead as to what is acceptable for me to say and do. At home, I can still call him by his pet name and tickle him on the couch."

It's a balancing act because you need to be yourself too. Dave is a jovial guy who plays with his kids and teases; it's his way of having fun. He wears his ugly cowboy shirt to answer the door and tells his daughters, "Don't squelch me and I won't squelch you." Teasing is a delicate matter. If everyone is enjoying it, it's okay; but if teasing hurts, it's cruel. If your teasing embarrasses or hurts your teenager, if he asks you to stop, then do, otherwise he'll feel he can't trust you.

Of course, you can't always avoid embarrassing your teenager, but never do it on purpose. Be considerate, treat them politely, use your manners. Never humiliate or shame. They won't be embarrassed by you forever, but for now you must definitely be sensitive.

Build a Bond of Camaraderie

When your child was younger, you knew more clearly what your role entailed. But now that your child is a teenager, it's easy to flounder around as you attempt to define your new relationship. In general, you want to balance head-of-the-household with the more subtle approach of friendship without crossing over the line into trying to be your child's friend. You both need to remember that you are not friends.

Adrian, fifteen years old, said it best: "I can tell my mom anything and I trust her with my feelings. We have a good relationship, but I don't consider our relationship a friendship. Even though I can talk to my mom about my life, she doesn't talk to me as much about hers. She keeps things from me; she doesn't tell me everything. It's better for her to share those things with her friends."

It's not appropriate for your son or daughter to know all the details of your life—some burdens are too heavy for them to bear. Elliot, fourteen, said he hated it when his divorcing parents confided in him. Kim said she didn't want to hear about her mother's romances. Joshua, seventeen, doesn't think teenagers should know the details of their parents arguments. He thinks that if parents have personal problems, they should talk them over with their own friends, not with their kids.

A friendship is a relationship between people based on trust and interests. Although you and your daughter might have a lot in common, you still have a distinct relationship. You have given birth, raised, and nurtured your daughter; you have been her guardian and protector. That makes you more than friends—after all, you'll always be her parent just as she'll always be your child.

The good news is that even though you aren't friends per se, you can be friendly toward each other. Friendliness is a quality, a style of relating. You and your child are allies—you have a permanent connection, you share the same struggles, the same victories. If his heart is broken, so is yours.

You can build a bond of camaraderie in little ways each day: a friendly "hello," when they come home, amiable banter over breakfast, sharing a piece of information, chatting about their day, or supporting their interests. Tim, fifteen, likes to build computers, so his dad picks up second-hand monitors and keyboards and brings them home. When thirteen-year-old Morgan was sick in bed for a week, her mom put a vase of flowers in her room to cheer her up. By doing something nice for your teen, you're showing that you're thinking of her and that you care. By doing these things, you're establishing a sense of compatibility, understanding, and rapport—the basis for harmony, equanimity, cooperation, and teamwork. Your friendliness toward them reaps friendliness in return.

Encourage Activities to Let Off Steam

It's normal for teenagers to lounge around occasionally; they need to "veg out." After all, growth spurts and mood swings use up lots of physical and emotional energy. Staring into space, or soaking up the sun may be a good way to recover, but it's not meant to be a way of life. A teenager lying on the couch day after day is bored, perhaps depressed, and badly in need of outlets for her energies. Guiding your teenager as he learns to balance work and play, responsibilities and goofing off, is another challenge you'll face. The trick is to know when to intervene.

Although it's necessary for teenagers to have free time, it's important that they balance that downtime with energetic activities, sports, creative projects, and some old-fashioned work. Having too much to do leads to premature burn-out in teenagers; on the other hand, being lazy and idle makes them sluggish, lethargic, and apathetic.

When Kelly finished her very active junior year, she slept past noon when summer vacation came. Although tempted, Pam didn't say much because she knew Kelly needed to get caught up on her rest, but still she was concerned: Would this become a habit? Would she turn into a slug? The condition wasn't permanent. After a couple weeks of sleeping in, Kelly found a summer job as a lifeguard.

Martin and Cecila felt apprehensive when Jon, seventeen, showed no motivation to get a summer job. Martin said, "He worked so hard during the school year that I thought it might be better not to have a rigorous schedule." Cecila said, "I wasn't sure, but I agreed as long as he wasn't lying around the house." That summer, Jon went to camp and did odd jobs for the neighbors. Martin and Cecila felt that things worked out okay because Jon was eager to go back to school and get a job the following summer.

Many kids get into trouble if they are allowed too much unstructured time. Fourteen-year-old Romona spent an entire summer watching soap operas. Whenever Linda complained or suggested an activity, Romona snapped so loudly that Linda backed down. Soon she was hanging.around with a fast crowd, staying out late at night, and sleeping most of the day. Rory, thirteen, was so bored that he hung around the park, smoking cigarettes all day. When his grandfather Roger found out, he put Rory to work cleaning the garage. Then Roger gave him a choice of summer activities: Rory choose skateboard day camp, drum lessons, and washing the family cars.

Whereas it seldom works to coerce an unwilling teen into a particular activity, teenagers do respond to choices. Amber agreed to organize the family photo albums during summer vacation. In the afternoons, she played tennis; in the evenings, she was with friends.

When you give him a project that helps you out, you're instilling pride and a sense of accomplishment. When you encourage activities to let off steam, you're keeping her interested in life.

Guide Them Toward Their Passion

On career day in Amanda's sophomore year in high school, a teacher asked her what career she wanted to pursue. Amanda answered, "I want to be a cultural anthropologist." The teacher responded with, "You can't do that—there aren't any jobs for cultural anthropologists." Horrified, Amanda came home and told me what the teacher had said. We talked it over and concluded that the teacher, although she meant well, was stuck with limited, self-defeating thinking. We prefer to use possibility thinking to make our dreams come true. Perhaps Amanda can become a cultural anthropologist by creating her own job. Who knows what's possible?

Sometimes we set limitations for our teenagers by saying, "That's not possible," when it would be more encouraging to say, "Maybe it is possible." If you are always telling your teenagers, "You can't do that," they will feel defeated before they start, and lose their motivation. It's wiser to say, "I think you could," or "Maybe you can."

Encourage your teens to find something they enjoy doing and cheer them on. Overnight success is a myth. There are many small steps that lead up to "overnight success," steps no one can see. One step leads to the next, with many turns and detours in the road. You may not know for sure where you are going, and may never reach the places you were heading for, but you'll usually end up somewhere better than you'd planned. One thing leads to something else; one opportunity taken brings another.

Teens become strong as they identify their talents and use them diligently. It takes some people until middle age or later to discover and deploy their gifts, but that doesn't mean they aren't gifted. We all know adults who have careers they really don't like, because they were never encouraged to find their true talent or because they thought it would please their parents to follow in their footsteps.

Learning to follow your own talents and gifts, doing what you love, following your dreams is more satisfying then doing what someone else thinks is best. Tell your kids, "With a little talent, a lot of hard work, and doing what you love, you're certain to be successful." It's when you do what you think you *should* do, that you become average, mediocre.

What do your teens love to do? When you help them visualize their dreams, they'll see beyond the accepted ways of doing things. Encourage your teenagers by letting them be who they are meant to be. Help them dream big.

Honor Their Wild, Strong, and Free Nature

If you've ever been to an amusement park and looked at the faces of the folks in line, you know that teenagers like anything that packs a kick, a bang, a wallop. It's normal for your teenager to want excitement and thrills. Like young racehorses at the starting gate, they're ready to run. I'm sure you've noticed that racehorses and teenagers get antsy when fenced in too long. Teenagers want to be wild, to sow some oats.

If you were deprived of fun as a child, you might be jealous of their enthusiasm, the sparkle in their eye, the spring in their step. Some adults try to squelch teenagers' mischievousness. They don't like their jaunty walk, their impish attitude. Perhaps it's because, as Jeanine, age sixteen, philosophized, "they were once 'goody-goodies' and didn't have much fun. Or they were 'bad-bad' boys and know what they did, so they're worried their kids will do the same." Fourteen-year-old Parker thinks it's because "parents want other parents to think their own kids are perfect."

It's true that some adults prefer kids to be goody-goodies. By insisting only on the best behavior, they repress and deny the dark side, the shadow that lurks in all of us, giving us depth and character and adding balance to our lives.

Freedom to be spontaneous teaches your daughter about herself. She's responding to a natural inclination, an urge from within. Boys being loud and rowdy are letting off steam, working off pent-up energy. It's not harmful but it makes adults uptight. Unrestrained play, jumping, laughing, saying shocking and scandalous things are other ways kids express their freedom.

Some parents think *wild and crazy* means destructive, but it isn't necessarily so. Kids who are destructive probably have something else going on. Teens do play pranks, but they're seldom more harmful than soggy toilet paper on the trees.

Child development experts tell us that this "wild and crazy" stage is significant because it helps teens resolve the inner conflicts of good and evil. In the end, good wins, but your teenager must arrive at this conclusion on her own. She must not be manipulated into being good because you demand it, but rather because she chooses to be. By acting out, she learns to control her impulses. So let her be sassy and free; it's the chance to work this out before the demands of adulthood set in.

Teens need lots of fun, otherwise how can they settle down, take on adult responsibilities, and focus on their careers? People who don't sow their wild oats are bitter, resentful, and old before their time. People in the know have told me: "Teens who didn't get to blow off steam or let out their wild streak have midlife crises and buy little red sports cars."

Let Them Burn
the Midnight Oil

Parents are tired and I think I know why. Once you have a kid, your natural sleeping pattern is disturbed or interrupted for at least the next nineteen years.

Remember when your teenager was a sweet baby, up at the crack of dawn and wanting to be fed? You were convinced you'd never get to sleep late again and you longed for just one more hour in bed. Remember when you wanted her to go to bed early so you could get caught up on the chores and have quiet time for yourself? All you wanted was a little peace and quiet to unwind, read, or talk with your spouse. So you worked to establish a routine; and just when you won the bedtime battle, suddenly she's a teen, and you realize you're *still* not going to sleep a full eight hours.

Now your teen stays out late, and you're tired because you can't fall asleep until she's home safe. You tell her to come home early because, "I worry," and she looks at you as if you're crazy and advises, "I'll be okay—go to sleep." So you toss and turn, trying to remember what's so fun about staying out late.

For years, Rudy liked to stay awake until midnight; now at age fifteen, he prefers to be with friends until 2 A.M. on weekends. His mother says, "I'd rather have them awake in the house than on the streets. It's okay as long as I know exactly where he is. They're not doing anything unusual—just playing Ping-Pong, throwing popcorn around the basement."

When Todd complained that his curfew was too early, Jean and George asked him what he suggested. He wanted to set his own curfew. They agreed, so long as they knew where he was and when he'd be home, and that he came home when he said he would. That way they'd know when they could get to sleep.

Amanda has never had a curfew imposed by me. Our agreement is that if she's out late, she calls at midnight and again right before she starts home so I know when to expect her.

No one knows for sure why kids like to burn the midnight oil, but it's a fact that they do. Perhaps it's a symbol of privilege and freedom. Your kids will probably do as Todd and Amanda do—go through a late, late period until the novelty wears off and the tiredness sets in; then they come home early and go to bed.

Share the Car

Remember the good ol' days when you worried that your precious toddler would run into the street and get hit by a car? She was small enough so you could hold her hand as you warned her to look both ways. She learned to cross the street, but you still worried that she wouldn't pay attention. Remember when your nine year old started riding his bike and doing wheelies? You insisted he wear a helmet, which he did, most of the time, yet sometimes he'd forget. Remember how relieved you felt each time he came home safe?

Perhaps it's surviving those times that prepares you for the terror ahead, as you let him take the wheel of your car for the first time.

Driving a car is a big deal—after all, we're a society that values cars as a symbol of adulthood and success. With a set of wheels, your teenager is mobile; he can get around without depending on you for a ride, and it's a relief for you too, because you're no longer the taxi driver.

Everyone handles "the car thing" differently. Some give their kids a new car the day they turn sixteen, others let them buy their own junker; some parents contribute to the insurance, others share the family car. There's no one way to do things, but, if you're not careful, "the car" can become another battleground. Greg said, "My dad uses the truck he gave me to control me; if I don't do exactly what he wants, he threatens to take the truck away." Molly added, "The only fights my dad and I have are over when I can use the car."

Although it's true that withholding car privileges may be the only control you feel you have over your teenager, it's best to establish a relationship wherein you can talk problems through rather than resort to threats of taking the car away. There are those times, however, when it does work to confiscate the keys.

"We tried to talk with Max about coming home at a reasonable hour, but he wasn't cooperating, so we got fed up and took the keys for one week. After having to hitch rides with friends, he must have understood that we meant business, because it hasn't been an issue since," said a relieved mother.

The privilege of getting a license and driving the car can be a powerful motivation for teens who are not living up to their responsibilities. Let them know what you expect and what the reward will be.

So give them lessons. Take them with you in the car and let them drive; and when you're scared to death, remember that you have to let them grow sometime. Soon the tables are turned, and they're telling *you* how to drive and that they're afraid to ride with *you*. Sixteen-year-old Rosie says, "The biggest problem I have is when Mom slams her feet on the floor as if she's putting on the brake, or when she holds on to the armrest as I turn the corner. I don't know why she does that; I'm a better driver than she is."

Isn't it crazy? You've driven for twenty years, and they've driven for twenty days, and they're already advising you. At least you're not a chauffeur anymore.

Find Healthy Ways
to Be High

We hear a lot of talk these days about drugs and alcohol. Indeed it's of concern to all of us. Today's newspaper headline screams that marijuana use among teens has doubled in the past decade. Families and communities are grappling with what to do. Let's face it, the war on drugs and "just say no" have failed to solve the problem. As concerned parents, we must stop and ask ourselves if we have faced the underlying issues.

Why do our children do drugs and drink? Is it because we do? Marisa, fourteen, gets drunk on the weekends. She doesn't consider it a problem because, she says, "My parents drink every day." Jon, the father of two, has been smoking pot since his twenties, but he's says, "My kids don't know." Here again, it's our *behavior* our kids our picking up on, not our lectures.

Why do kids and adults want to be high? Folks using drugs regularly are trying to cope with feelings that make them uncomfortable, and teens in trouble are acting out feelings they don't understand. Although experimentation doesn't necessarily mean you'll get hooked, and smoking as a teenager doesn't mean you'll smoke as an adult, still, it's chancy.

Science has shown there is something in our brain that craves highs—but they don't need to be drug-induced. It's better for you and your kids to imbibe on positive highs. Some of the most alive experiences come from sleeping under starlight, trampling through woods, sitting on a mountain, wading in a creek, floating down a river. Sometimes we are most at home in nature, listening to the songs of birds. No one can stay cranky out of doors; your thoughts and worries vanish when you soak up fresh air. Everything's in harmony. That's a natural high.

If you've ever sang around a campfire, you know the thrill of belonging that ran through your veins. If you've roasted hotdogs and ate s'mores, you know the ecstasy of simple living. Send your teen to summer camp or let the gang go camping. I took Amanda to Bali to soak in another culture and to open her eyes to something more—to the world at large. She says it was "heaven." When you expose your kids to folks beyond your front door, you expand their minds in ways no drug can.

The best way to sustain a natural high is to feel good about yourself. Experts tell us that high self-esteem makes the difference for teenagers. Do what you can to accentuate the positive. If you're pessimistic or depressed, it's bound to rub off on your kids. If you're down in the dumps and critical, if you can't say anything good, its sets a tone of gloom that might not wear off. Look for the silver lining, whistle while you work. When you're upbeat and cheerful, your son or daughter is optimistic and doesn't need to drink to get high. Drugs and alcohol make your energy chaotic; love and optimism lifts everyone up.

Take Every Opportunity to Hang Out

The best bridge for the generation gap is to appreciate your teenager as a person with her own thoughts and feelings and to let her know you as an individual. So often we see one another just in our roles. Your teenager views you as the parent; you view your teenager as the child. This one-dimensional view of one another causes a rift—each side assuming they know exactly what the other is going to do or say—and creates a generation gap which for some families takes years to bridge.

The quickest way to get reacquainted with one another is to hang out together—not with any purpose in mind, not to force conversation, but to be together as people, not as parent, not as child. In an ambiance of pressure-free, unstructured time, you have the opportunity to see each other in a new light. When the Sanchez family tied two large hammocks to trees in the backyard, Maria noticed that her fourteen-year-old son, Juan, and her husband, Dan, could "hang" side by side without arguing. Dan said, "We enjoy staring into space."

This isn't always easy to do. One dad told me: "I feel there has to be a message when I talk to my son. I worry that if we just hang out, I'm not doing my job." Now that his son is nineteen and has moved out of the house, they can't get together without tension. "There's a gulf between us." He would like to let go of his parental role, but it's such a habit; he wishes they could have fun and relax.

To hang out with your teenager, look for the small opportunities, a break from your regular routine, to seize the moment and be together. If you make elaborate plans, you're likely to be disappointed, because teenagers often resist overt attempts to have "quality time." But if you're aware of those instances when neither of you is feeling pressured, you'll be able to relax, unwind, and enjoy a minute or more of serenity, and the gap between you will lessen.

Hanging out can happen in the backyard, the kitchen, or the car. It can be a few minutes or an entire day. The key is to drop expectations, roles, rules, and notions about what is "supposed" to happen. Hanging out means being together, sharing a moment in sweet accord—it's those moments of doing nothing, solving nothing, that blesses your relationship.

Hanging out is good for families who want to stay together, or, as one fourteen year old put it: "If you want your family to hang in during the tough times, then hang out."

Security

There's never any reason to throw your teen out of your heart—not even for a moment. When you believe in them wholeheartedly, they learn to believe in themselves.

Believe in Them Totally

Think back to your own adolescence and ask yourself if at any time during those years did you feel troubled or discouraged. Was your heart broken? Did you think you didn't belong or wonder if you would ever fit in? Were you ever filled with sadness or self-doubt? Did you feel confused or hopeless with no place to turn? Or did you have someone to talk with, to confide in, to help you out?

Who was that person? Who believed in you even though you had lost belief in yourself? Who was there for you when you needed a shoulder to cry on? When you longed for a comforting hug? Was it a friend, a teacher, a parent, a grandparent, a coach, or a stranger? Who saw the spark of potential within you and said, "I know you can do it!"?

If you were fortunate to have one person who recognized the scope of who you were, and who showed you the way, you know how important that backing was. If you had no one at your side, you know what you missed—how alone you felt—and you don't want your own teenager to have such a struggle.

Your belief that your teenager is capable and intrinsically good is a prerequisite for the development of a responsible and enthusiastic young adult. He needs you to believe this totally! He needs you to believe in him even when he makes bad choices, when he lets you down and disappoints you. He needs you to believe in him, to love him, to never give up on him. If you stop believing in him, he will have a very hard time getting on track again. Even when your teenager's behavior is less than desirable, when he does something foolish, uses poor judgment, or completely messes up, remember that he does it because often it is the only choice he thought he had at the moment.

Every teenager will mess up, take risks, get in trouble, break a rule, try to get away with something, and keep something from you. Some kids will get in legal scrapes, causing all kinds of chaos. Even so, when she gets into a big mess, keep your focus on the larger picture—reminding yourself over and over that the trouble she is having is only a small part of who she is. Let your teenager know, that even though she's made mistakes, you still believe in her totally. Only then will she be able to learn from her mistakes, correct them, and move on.

Believing that your teenager is a wonderful person who will succeed becomes a self-fulfilling prophecy for him. If you believe in him no matter what, even when he has lost belief in himself he can turn his life around.

Admire Who They Are, as They Are

Have you ever experienced being loved by a brother, sister, parent, or grandparent, even though you were acting cruel, angry, or mean? Have you seen the twinkle and delight in your grandparents' eyes and known they loved you no matter what. When you felt inadequate, defective, or inferior, did someone in your family—perhaps an aunt, an uncle, or a cousin—look at you with so much compassion that your worries and doubts melted away?

If you've had the fortune of knowing unconditional love from your family, you know that you are blessed. If you've longed for the warmth of deep, abiding familial love, if you sensed that something is amiss because you've never had it, you don't want your teenager to ache from such emptiness.

Can you love your son or daughter without conditions? Without conditions doesn't mean without demands. Sometimes we do need to make some demands on our teens. That's very normal and natural. And we can withhold rewards from them too—sometimes that's necessary to get them to do what we expect. We can withhold the amount of time we spend with them or how much attention we give them. We can keep the car keys, deduct from their allowance, or ground them for a weekend. But we should not withhold our love.

We may get angry at them, but we should not close our hearts to them. We must find ways to honor them even when they disappoint us. We can clash on many issues—so long as our love for them is not an issue. When teens are supported, they thrive, and we all benefit. Teenagers who are appreciated are eager to learn and be involved.

There are many stereotypes about teenagers that fill us with trepidation. Parents, teachers, and other adults are influenced by the negative publicity teenagers get. In fact, some folks become so alarmed by seeing a group of teenagers walking down the street that they automatically assume, as one security guard told me, that "teens are up to no good."

Unfortunately, this assumption influences how we treat teenagers in our homes, our schools, and our communities. When we think of teens as aimless, irresponsible troublemakers, we don't have the patience or compassion for them that they need. If we think of them as worthless, we don't take time to teach them what they need to know.

Such a poisonous attitude toward the upcoming generation eats away at our collective spirit, leaving us pessimistic, cynical, and ineffective. With a cloud of gloom and doom permeating the adult/teen relationship, it's no wonder that teens often feel deserted.

Teens need parents who are public-relations experts focused on how well so many of them are coping with the daily challenges of their fast-paced, demanding world. They need your admiration now—they need to know that you cherish them, that you take delight in who they are, and that you're willing to spread the word.

Behave Respectfully

If you want your teenager to respect you, *you* must behave respectfully. The chain of respect starts with you and travels downward to your teenager. Be alert to your own actions and demeanor, because your words and behavior are influencing your teen. This means you treat *everyone* in the household with dignity, love, and compassion. If you, the mother, want your daughter to respect her father, you must model acceptable behavior by your own actions toward him. If you, the father, want your son to respect his mother, you must behave respectfully toward her yourself. It's by your example that you teach teenagers respect for themselves, for others, and for you.

Almost all parents blow up at their kids, freak out, or attack—at least occasionally. Teenagers' behavior can sometimes be so maddening, outlandish, and infuriating that even a saint would lose patience. Even so, you set the tone for respect by the way you treat your teenagers each and every moment—even when they're driving you crazy.

There are many opportunities within your family to show respect for one another. You show respect when you listen carefully to what family members have to say. You show respect when you follow through with what you said you'd do, when you take into consideration each other's feelings, when you go out of your way to do something thoughtful, when you notice the look on the other's face that says I'm *having a hard day* and you respond with kindness.

When you treat your teenager the way *you* want to be treated, you are practicing the Golden Rule: Do unto your teenager as you would have your teenager do unto you. This means no name-calling or put-downs, no poking fun or ridiculing, no subtle innuendoes or sarcasm. It means not jumping to conclusions by assuming the worst.

Adam, fourteen, postponed mowing the lawn until the last minute before leaving for the baseball tournament. His dad, Gerald, could tell by the ragged edges that the job was done in a hurry, but instead of yelling, criticizing, and calling Adam names, as his own father did to him, he spoke calmly yet firmly: "I noticed that the yard needs more work, especially in the front, and the mower needs to be put away. When can you do it?" With such respect from his dad, Adam jumped up from his chair and completed the task. Unfortunately, in some families the same scenario could have ruined an entire evening with the father shaming his son, or arguing, fighting, and calling each other names.

What you do and what you say does matter. You set the standard.

Let Them Learn
by Experience

We all know that experience is a good teacher, and if you want your teenager to gain from her own experience, you must be patient rather than punitive. Here's a personal story to illustrate what I mean: Whenever I warned Amanda that she was driving too fast, she countered with: "I know what I'm doing, Mom," or, "You drive too fast, too," or, "No, I'm not," and so on. She'd slow down for a while but, in spite of my best efforts, she'd soon be speeding again. Then one day, just as I predicted, she got a ticket, and I was tempted to tell her "I told you so." I had to fight back the urge to deliver a well-deserved lecture, but since I had previously warned her of all the ramifications of speeding, I decided this time to be patient and see what would happen.

Amanda wanted to pay the fine from her savings, but I suggested nonchalantly (which was not easy) that we go to court and see if she could get the fine reduced or erased from her record. I knew she would learn many lessons, on many different levels, from this speeding ticket and appearing in court.

I was careful not to scare her by making court an intimidating event. I didn't want her fear to be all-consuming, because that would prevent her from facing the consequences of her actions. So I stood by her side and told her, "I know you can do it."

When we walked into the courtroom, she understood for the first time that she had to talk in front of a roomful of other traffic violators. She listened as people told their stories filled with all kinds of excuses. She was getting more and more nervous, so I whispered: "You'll do fine."

When the clerk called her name, she stood up, walked to the bench, looked directly at the judge, and spoke respectfully, clearly, and honestly, explaining the circumstances. The judge asked a few questions, then reduced the fine and, since it was a first offense, cleared her record. She sighed with relief and thanked me for helping her.

I was proud of her. She handled herself responsibly under pressure. I know she learned from this experience, because her driving is better, and I think she gained competence in her ability to handle adult situations. I was proud of myself too, that with just a little patience, we both learned from experience, which turned out much better than scolding, threatening, or acting like the judge myself.

Have Faith in Their Ability to Find Solutions

Your parental objective is to teach your teenager responsibility for her life. To achieve this, she must practice making her own decisions, coming up with her own solutions. She won't accomplish this if you're continually taking over and running the show.

Your teenager will face many challenges and temptations. Even if you could always be there, it's not wise to solve all her problems, control her every move, or to try to sway her to do it your way. When you continuously run her life, you foster unhealthy dependency, and, as a result, your daughter might never learn to take charge. When you try to run the show, she rebels, becomes uncooperative, makes poor choices, and gives you a hard time.

Cynthia tried to control fifteen-year-old Zack by commenting on his choices. When he got a mohawk haircut, she poked fun at him; when he wanted an earring, she objected so strongly that he went behind her back and got a tattoo. When she refused to let him play football because she thought it was too dangerous, he started smoking pot. When she openly criticized his friends, he started lying. Her controlling backfired with his rebellion.

From something as simple as what outfit to wear or what class to take, to something more significant such as to whether to cut class on Friday, your teenager is fighting for independence. The first step toward achieving this is making his own choices, finding his own solutions, making his own way. Brad, the father of two teenage boys, told me, "When it comes to my kids, I think I have to find the solutions, but I know it's better to trust them to find their own."

Michael could see that his son, Graham, a junior in high school, put so much pressure on himself to get good grades that he would sometimes freeze during an exam. Whenever Michael tried to offer a suggestion about relaxing, Graham would get more uptight. "By talking about the problem, I was making matters worse, so I decided to trust that Graham would come up with his own solution. I told him, 'I know you'll figure it out.'"

The wise parent puts himself in the background and lets his teenager make the choices. He encourages independence by saying: "It's your choice . . . Whatever you decide is fine . . . I trust you to make the best decision." A prudent parents offers assistance by saying, "If you want my help to figure it out, let me know."

Your abiding faith gives her courage to keep going, even when times are tough, when she's discouraged and wants to give up. By your believing in her, she confidently faces whatever life brings her way. Your faith keeps her believing in herself; your assurance is powerful motivation. She wants you to know she's independent and capable; your faith reassures her that she is.

Plant the Seeds
of Suggestions

When conversations with your teenager become impossible because she thinks she knows more than you do, when he doesn't want to talk about it and clams up, or if one of you is yelling, it's time to test a potent remedy: Plant a suggestion seed, stand back, and watch it grow.

None of us likes to be told what to do; it's human nature to bristle when someone tells you how to manage your life. Even when you do ask for advice, you usually don't want to be told exactly what to do—you want to figure it out for yourself. This is especially true for your teenager.

Think about how many adults at school or in extracurricular activities are telling your teenager what to do. When you think of it this way, you'll realize how much she really is cooperating; it's noteworthy how well she handles all the advice, orders, and rules. By the end of the day, she's probably saturated with so much counsel that it's no wonder she gets defensive with more well-intentioned guidance from you.

Planting a suggestion seed lets your child think about things without having to decide on the spot. It's giving a hint at the options you hope she'll consider, without forcing. When Chloe was thinking about joining the soccer team, her dad said in passing, "Have you considered going out for track? You might think about it; you have real talent and you could be eligible for a scholarship." Then he walked away. When Josh had no luck finding a summer job, Marge suggested, "Have you thought about talking with Uncle Hank? He knows lots of people." Clarice used the same approach when talking with her son about buying his first car: "You might want to get a quote on insurance costs before you commit."

Wisely, these parents planted their suggestions but didn't lecture, nag, or grumble, which made it possible for the seeds to grow. Chloe did join the track team, Josh worked for his uncle Hank, and Doug postponed his car purchase.

If confronting directly brings out defensiveness in your teen, try planting casual suggestions for faster results. Bill wasn't sure he liked the idea of Jason going hiking in the bad weather and said, "If you don't mind getting cold and wet, you'll have fun." Jason thought about it for a while and announced, "I'm not going in the rain."

Your responsibility as a parent is to give them the information, tell them about the things they may not have thought of, and let them work it out. When you plant a suggestion seed, your teenager can mull over your idea, modify it, and claim it as her own. Then everyone reaps the harvest.

Stand Back and Watch Them Grow

When you plant a suggestion seed, don't expect results right away. In a garden, you know you'll have to wait for the seeds to sprout, and coaxing won't hurry the process. Seeds in your garden must be watered, fed, and cared for daily or they will not sprout, mature, and thrive. It's identical with your teenager. Even though you can't see the results for weeks, maybe months, they still need to be fed and given friendly attention. So if you want your suggestions to grow, be patient, devoted, loyal, and caring. Watch and wait.

Fourteen-year-old Chad was flunking math. His mother knew from past experience that threatening, scolding, and lecturing never produced positive results, so this time she tried planting a suggestion seed. "You might consider asking your teacher for the name of a tutor. I'd be willing to pay for one. Let me know; it's up to you." Then she waited for six days—still feeding him, hanging out with him, and carefully avoiding harping before she Inquired, "What did you decide about hiring a tutor? Can I be of assistance?" Chad mumbled, "Yup. Would you call the teacher and get one?" "Good idea—I'll be glad to." Her suggestion seed took root and grew. Mom was relieved and Chad saved face.

The Logans had three children of their own when their sixteen-year-old niece, Janey, came to live with them. Janey was obstinate, depressed, and stubborn. She wasn't doing anything at school except hanging out with undesirable friends. Nothing the Logans said or did made any difference until they asked Janey, "What do you want to do after you graduate?" Janey answered, "Get an apartment and live on my own." They thought she'd never be able to support herself, but kept their skepticism to themselves and instead said, "Great!" and asked, "Would you like us to help you design a plan-for-independence?"

That was the first of many suggestion seeds they planted over the next two years. The plan-for-independence was the seed that grew. It took root when Janey made a list of what she needed to know to be independent by graduation. A personalized plan-for- independence was the motivation she needed. Over the next two years, the Logans were persistent in directing her focus back to her plan.

A plan-for-independence seed might work for you too, but remember that *all* seeds won't take root. But if you plant a wide variety, some will bloom beautifully.

Admit When You're Angry

Over the next few years, you're bound to get angry, fed up, disgusted, frustrated, annoyed, and downright furious with your teenager. So you might as well admit it! It's best to let them know openly rather than let them absorb your hostile vibes. As one mom told me, "I admit it—I'm irked!"

It's not healthy for a teenager to live with a martyr mother who pretends "it doesn't matter," by smiling sweetly on the outside while feeling enraged on the inside. It's not healthy for a teenager to be with a long-suffering father who feels taken advantage of by his kids, but ignores it and withdraws. On the other hand, neither it is healthy for anyone to live in a household where members explode in violent, angry rages. If the layer of fury is so thick around your house that your teenager has to tiptoe on eggshells to avoid your wrath, you need to learn to turn your anger into a productive rather than a harmful force.

When you're angry, don't ignore it or you'll make matters worse. By being too kind, too patient, and too understanding, you convey a wishy-washy hypocrisy that creates an unhealthy turmoil in you and your teenager. They'll take advantage of your good nature and feel guilty. When you ignore what's bothering you, eventually you'll explode, making a scene out of proportion to the "crime," and then you'll feel guilty. After pushing his son's head against the kitchen wall, Mark said, "I got so mad, I was shaking. I've tried ignoring what he's doing, but this time I lost it." A vicious circle—nothing solved.

Remember, anger is a sign that something's wrong. Teenagers need limits; they need to know when "enough is enough." They need you to put your foot down. Use your anger to let them know clearly how their behavior is affecting you. Don't call them names or attack, simply let them know where you stand.

Jamie, fifteen, was demanding, sullen, and surly. When she wanted money for clothes, makeup, lunch, or the movies, she expected her mom to give it to her. She did absolutely nothing around the house; her room was a mess, her belongings strung all over. She begged for piano lessons, but sulked when reminded to practice. As Jamie slouched on the couch with her feet on the coffee table, instead of screaming "What's the matter with you—don't you know any better?" her mother changed her tactics. She described what she saw, how it made her feel, and what she wanted done: "When I see your feet on the table, I get furious! Your feet belong on the floor." Then she continued this approach with the room, the money, and the lessons. Instead of insulting and threatening, she used her anger to make her wishes known. And it worked!

Refine the Knack of Arguing

Arguing goes with the teenage turf. I once asked a seasoned grand-mother of fourteen if she and her kids ever argued. "Yes," she smiled. "We did, but not nearly as much as we should have." She reminded me of an important finding—that the way a family deals with conflict is the single most important factor in keeping the family close.

There are many negative ways to deal with conflict. You can pre-tend it doesn't exist or you can overpower your teen—whether physi-cally or with a bribe. No conflicts will ever arise if you buy your teen enough gifts and if you ignore anything negative.

I know a father who doesn't even hear remarks he doesn't want to hear. He's convinced that anything that may lead to friction must be tuned out and insists that everyone do as he says and like it. If anyone complains, he just doesn't hear it. I also know a mother who smiles no matter what. Both of them are right—up to a point. Avoiding needless skirmishes is one of the talents of raising a teen, but you can't continu-ally sweep genuine conflict under the rug. It will eventually bubble up somehow. Conflict needs to be dealt with. If you don't deal with it, it gathers momentum until one day nothing can stop it, and it thunders down on you like an avalanche.

What does learning to deal with conflict mean? For one thing, un-derstand that family quarrels do not have to mean the end of the world or the end of your relationship. You and your kids can disagree and argue and get mad, and the love can still be there.

Some families, of course, don't fight. They live in perpetual harmony and my guess is that many of them are bored. They sit on pools of stagnant energy. They probably don't get very close to one another either. Closeness in a family sometimes seems to require arguing. There is nothing wrong with that so long as it results in growth and realization for you—some insight in understanding, in something constructive.

In every argument there is potential for learning. Something your teen says in haste and anger may hold a brilliant thread of truth that you've been overlooking. Use it to your advantage. The more you know about yourself, the more beautiful you'll feel. It's paradoxical that the more you address the underlying conflict, the more abiding peace you'll have.

Be Sensitive to Their Struggles

Life is not so simple for teens these days. Their schedules are hectic, their lives demanding. Erika, fourteen, points this out: "School is a much bigger pressure than most adults think. I put in seven and a half hours at school each day, followed by at least two hours of homework and two hours of swim team practice. I then have chores to do; sometimes I cook dinner because my mom works late. I don't have time to unwind or talk with friends. I think too much is expected of me and I feel pressured."

While they're juggling outside demands, emotionally they're sorting through the layers of self-doubt and turmoil. Paige, thirteen, says, "I want to have lots of friends, but I don't have the money to go to the movies or skating, so I get left out." Teens are also concerned about their personal appearance; they want to fit in, be popular. They may be dealing with the anguish of divorce, pressures to have sex, perhaps violence in their school or neighborhood.

Upset behavior and acting out are signals that something is amiss—something's wrong on the inside. When your teen is troubled, she might appear agitated, fidgety, absent-minded, or sullen. Instinctively, she knows she can't fix the outside without fixing the inside, so she turns inward. Lost in her inner thoughts and feelings, she's struggling to figure something out.

When you ask, "What's wrong?" teenagers frequently answer, "Nothing." It's not that they're trying to keep something from you, it's that they're really not sure. You've probably had the experience of feeling teary and didn't know why. You've probably felt shaky on the inside and haven't wanted to talk about what's upsetting you until you've mulled it over. Sometimes you've tried to hide it so people wouldn't notice and begin asking questions. It's the same for your teenager; he needs time to reflect on what's bothering him before he's ready to talk.

Your son or daughter needs you to be perceptive to this inner process. It's not your job to fix the problem; in fact, trying to give advice while they're upset only makes matters worse. Simply by being observant, you can notice the look on your daughter's face, the way your son hangs his head, that says I'm *having a bad day*. When your teenager is upset, behaving in ways you don't understand, it's probably because they're coping with feelings they don't fully comprehend either. A soft and patient look is all that's needed to let her know you're standing by. Your sensitive, gentle, kind-hearted nod can soothe more quickly than words.

Acquaint yourself with the issues your teen is facing. It's so comforting when a parent recognizes what a teenager has to deal with.

Acknowledge Their Choices

Your teens will not do everything the same as you. Hopefully, they will take the best of you, add to it, improve on it, and become who they are destined to be.

The search for autonomy—finding a personal identity—is the main emotional drive of a teenager. The very process of growing up is a discovery of *who* I *am*, separate from everyone else. This requires seeking a personal style. It's a little like buying a new pair of shoes: You try on a variety of styles and sizes to find the one that fits your foot and personality. Likewise, your teen tries on different identities until he finds the perfect match. And just like your teen wouldn't dream of wearing your shoes, he doesn't want to be a carbon copy of you—he wants his own identity. You don't take it personally if he refuses to buy shoes exactly like yours, so don't take it personally when he makes choices that differ from yours. Remember, he's defining himself through his choices.

If you're perplexed by his choices, don't worry. Just as shoes go out of style quickly, your teenager's choices are not carved in stone—he's young and will probably change his style many times over the next five to ten years—as you most likely have also.

If you're telling your teenager how to dress, talk, and walk, you have too much power. If he's listening to you, he's having an internal battle and he might have difficulty finding his own identity; and if he doesn't already, sooner or later he'll resent you.

Your teenager gains confidence by asserting himself and making choices different from yours. When you disapprove, although he might never let you know, he loses confidence. You'll have a closer relationship with your son if you let him make his own choices, if you let him assert his uniqueness—discover what makes him special.

Your teenager knows she's like you in many ways, but wants to find the little ways in which she is unique. So if you like tennis shoes, she'll probably prefer sandals, and if you want her to wear sandals, she's sure to want boots. Either way, tell her, "I trust you to make good choices," or "You can choose what's right for you."

Handle the Unmentionables

Teens are learning about love and sexuality—perhaps that's what makes us uncomfortable about these years. Teenagers are interested in dating and falling in love; they wonder if their feelings are normal. And although they may not be sexually active, you might feel uneasy about this natural inclination.

We see their sexual urges and we don't want our "babies" to think about it—let alone "do it." At the least, we hope they'll postpone "jumping into the ocean" as long as possible. It's easy to be so uncomfortable with the topic that we never discuss it or, on the other hand, we resort to delivering lectures that are promptly tuned out.

So how do you talk with teenagers about love, sex, birth control, body image, and all the other changes brought to the forefront at puberty? If you've never talked about sexual matters, even if you can muster up your courage, it probably isn't realistic to sit your son or daughter down and expect to have a talk. Instead, it's more practical to educate *yourself* first—then you'll be prepared to use the opportunities as they arise.

Andy, the father of a fourteen year old, said, "If my son wants to see a R-rated movie, I'll gladly take him. It gives us a spontaneous lead-in to talk about what we saw. On the ride home, I can tell him what I think; at least I know I've given him my input."

In my years of counseling and teaching, I can't remember hearing one time when kids learned something meaningful about sex from parents who sat them down for a talk. Mostly, they learn by observation and listening. They see parents kissing, they watch television, go to movies, see billboards, talk with friends, and read books. It's an ongoing learning process that is speeded up now.

You'll have many chances to open a discussion about values, feelings, intimacy, and love. We're bombarded daily with sexual messages. You can use one of these moments to talk about the unmentionables: safe sex, diseases, sexual abuse, intimacy. You can share your thoughts about love, sex, and friendship, how they are related, and what it means to be in love.

The teens I talk with tell me that lust doesn't dominate their relationships. They want to belong, eventually find a lifelong mate. And even though they're curious when they feel loved and close, they're willing to postpone becoming sexually active. Teach your teen about sex, love, and relationships by sharing your perspective as it comes up. Don't just leave it to others.

Include Them in Your Life

Although it might seem that your children are setting you aside by not including you in the details of their lives, this is definitely not the time to exclude them from yours. Don't kick them out of your life now. Teenagers want to belong, be a part of you, be included in your life.

If your life is hectic and family members seem to be going their separate ways, you'll have to make the extra effort to keep each other informed. If there are a lot of comings and goings in your household, try hanging a family calendar and log in commitments so everyone can see.

If you want to know where your children are, let them know where *you* are. Tell them your schedule—where you're going and when you'll be back. Call if you'll be late. Leave them a note when you can't tell them in person. Let them know how to reach you. I've met teenagers who don't know for sure what their parents do each day. Take your kids to your workplace; let them see you at the office. Once a year, Angelia takes her daughters to her favorite business luncheon spot to give them a peek at their mom's business world. In just two hours, the girls see a professional side of their mom that they might miss otherwise. With this new perspective, they gain respect for all she's doing.

Through understanding how you spend your day and how you manage your life, teenagers gain appreciation for what you do, for how hard you work to support the family. As they see what you've achieved, you'll gain their respect. When they see firsthand what you cope with, they'll have more understanding about what you've accomplished, what you've overcome, and that's a practical learning experience.

Show them what you do. You'll be strengthening your ties, and, even though you might not know it, you'll also be teaching time management.

Truthfully Share
Your Life Stories

Teenagers need you to be forthright and give straight, honest answers to their questions. A parent of integrity tells it like it is, even if it means exposing the dark skeletons you'd rather hide.

Their families considered it shameful that Roberta and Paul "had to get married," and advised them to "keep it a secret." On the wedding day, they vowed never to let the baby know. They married in haste, and for years they waffled and squirmed, lying about the date.

One morning in the kitchen, the baby, now a six-foot-tall seventeen year old, announced to his mom what they feared for so long: He knew. A cousin had spilled the beans. Shaking, she wailed, and, striving to make it all right, she pleaded, "We're so . . . happy we had you, can you ever forgive us?" The young man shrugged, "It's okay, Mom. I know you and Dad aren't perfect."

Stretching the truth is such a big burden. The details you're agonizing to hide invariably get let out of the bag. Covering up never works for very long. When your kids ask, it's best to tell the truth.

Sharing your life story lets your kids in on the family history. It gives them insight and clarifies why you do the things you do. It gives them empathy for your plight, compassion for your efforts. Through your stories, they see you as a person rather than a one-dimensional "parental unit." Lindsey said, "When my parents tell me stories about their childhood, they seem like real people, not just my parents." Nick added, "I can relate to my parents more when they tell me what they did as teenagers."

When you share your teenage struggles, your kids gain understanding of the common predicaments and find out that all is not lost. It gives them hope: You've survived and so will they. Thirteen-year-old Elliot was greatly relieved to learn that his dad had been bullied and teased because he, too, was dyslexic. It lessened Zoey's burden to learn that her mom had been chubby. It gave Andy a boost to find out how often his dad sat on the bench. And when Sallee discovered how many times her mom had lost before winning a swim meet, she found new courage to keep trying.

Sharing stories from your childhood gives you a common reference point. It takes you off your domineering pedestal and brings you down to earth. That's a solid place to meet.

Negotiate, Negotiate

With a teenager in the house, you'll have lots of chances to sharpen your negotiation skills. It's a fine opportunity to learn to settle disputes so that everyone triumphs. If you use negotiation, you'll get to know each other better and you'll both feel comfortable, even when you don't see eye-to-eye, and you will be able to face disagreements without crumbling.

Conflict is inevitable in any relationship, and particularly with a teenager who is in the process of forming his or her identity. To expect otherwise is to miss the chance to get to know each other better. Conflicts won't ruin your relationship unless you sweep them under the rug and pretend they don't exist. Expecting everything to run smoothly without misunderstandings breeds distance and fosters a pattern of relating that's superficial.

Fourteen-year-old Katie has already given up talking things over with her mother because, she says, "My mom gets so upset when I disagree with her, that it's better to keep my thoughts to myself. She doesn't know me anymore."

This doesn't mean you should try to work things out in the heat of the moment. If everyone is yelling, take a thirty-minute time-out before you start negotiating. Let your son know that you want to listen to how he feels, by saying, "I want to give you my full attention, so let's take a time-out and meet back here in thirty minutes." During this time-out, take some deep breaths, center yourself, and get unruffled. You'll want to listen fully to your son's point of view and share yours calmly, before you begin to negotiate.

Some parents like to demand obedience to hard-and-fast rules because it's easier to enforce rules than to negotiate. Firmly established rules strip you and your teenager of the learning that comes from debating the pros and cons of each unique situation.

Carly wanted to go to a concert, but her mother wasn't comfortable with the surroundings. Negotiations started with each of them telling what they were asking for and why it's so important. Her mother said, "It's important for me to feel that you will be physically safe." Carly responded, "It's important to me to feel that you can trust me to take care of myself in this situation." From this beginning, they were able to go on to figure out what would make Mom secure and Carly feel trusted.

Ask for your kids' suggestions: "Can you think of another solution?" "Any other ideas?" "What do you want me to do?" There's lifetime skill gained in learning to talk things over. Negotiating helps your teen think things through, take both persons' needs into account, and feel responsible for coming up with a solution. When you negotiate, you continue to build a bond while respecting your teen's individuality.

Keep your rules at home negotiable. It takes more time and effort to negotiate, but it's keeps your home life lively and spontaneous. There are plenty of rules elsewhere that we're all following.

Let Them Know You Care

Teenagers need large doses of compassion and tender loving care. We give them so much materially and financially that we think we've done enough, but a simple act of kindness, especially from you, is more healing and nourishing for their souls than another pair of jeans. When was the last time you went with him for a walk? When do you give her a hug? Have you told them lately, "I'm glad you're here, glad to know you, glad you're in my life!"?

Even though you can no longer rock him to sleep, bounce him on your knee, or tuck him in at bedtime, your teen still yearns for expressions of your love. He may be taller than you, and she may be smarter, but still they long for loving reassurance. Your daughter may seem apathetic, and your son might not respond openly, yet deep inside the question lurks: *Do my parents love me? Do they really care?* Your loving declarations, your hugs and kisses provide the comfort when you can't wipe their tears and make it all better.

Sometimes it is easy to forget just why we had children and why we still love them. Thirteen-year-old Amber said, "My mom doesn't say she loves me anymore." Teens need to hear It, as seventeen-year-old Daniel said: "I'd like my dad to say he loves me with words. Then I know for sure." So give a hug or a kiss on the check. Shout out loud, "I love you, take care!" as they're running out the door.

When they respond with a shrug and a blank stare, say it gently or write it. Don't expect affectionate words in return; teenagers can be embarrassed by exposing their sensitive feelings. Samantha, whose parents are divorced, says, "My dad writes me and tells me all the time that he loves me. I like it! I like knowing that he can say it even though I've never said it back. I don't know why I don't say it. I guess I'm embarrassed."

Show that you care by your actions too. Tony works nights and sleeps days, so he misses out on family dinners and daily gossip. Feeling left out and wanting to catch up on the latest happenings, he scheduled a Sunday morning 7 A.M. breakfast gathering and asked his kids to come. His thirteen year old grumbled loudly, the fifteen year old pouted, the eighteen year old sighed grudgingly, and the nineteen year old refused. So Tony made attendance mandatory. Skeptical, his wife set the table in style while Tony whipped up his famous omelets. He told the kids, "I miss seeing my family—you're the most important people in my life. I want to know what's going on in your lives. I want to keep in touch." In spite of the initial grumblings, they had a good time.

Write your teen a testimonial letter, read it aloud, or send him a copy. Be specific about what you see in him, what qualities you admire. Give her hugs in private. Tell him you'll always be there for him. They need to know this now.

Establish Guidelines That Inspire

Teenagers frequently find themselves boxed in with so many rules and unspoken instructions that they don't have an opportunity to think for themselves. Parents and authority figures repeatedly use their power over teens to get them to do it the proscribed way. Power tactics ultimately backfire because the teenager either rebels and tries to get away with something or, at the other extreme, quietly acquiesces and never learns to think for herself.

We want our teenagers to be able to think on-the-spot and make good decisions on the spur of the moment when we aren't around. Ultimately, we want them to rule themselves, and to do that they need to learn to think for themselves. So set guidelines that inspire your teenager to think the consequences through, use good judgment, and make meaningful choices.

Here's an example: When Nicholas was fifteen, he sneaked out at midnight to go to a friend's house. He knew that if his parents woke up and found him gone, they'd freak out, so wisely he wrote a note, telling them where he'd be, and taped it in such a way that when he returned he'd know immediately if his parents had seen it. He made it back before sunrise; finding the note undisturbed, he was relieved. A neighbor saw him climbing in the window, however, and told this parents. Initially, they felt that the wool had been pulled over their eyes and paced the floor in a frenzy. When they calmed down, they could see that he had exercised good judgment by leaving the note, so they choose to use the rational approach.

Without shaming, blaming, threatening, scolding, or screaming, they let Nicholas explain his actions. They put themselves in his shoes, listened, understood his thinking, and saw his point of view. It was a collaborative effort. Nicholas and his parents established a new guideline for such situations: If Nick felt it necessary to be with friends, instead of sneaking out he would tell his parents directly that "this is really important," and they wouldn't interfere. If they felt such a guideline was being taken advantage of, they reserved the right to renegotiate.

Rules need to allow for the unexpected—the movie getting out late or friends in crisis needing to talk. So when your teenager calls you to tell you she'll be home late, don't lower the boom like one father did, grounding her anyway. Allow your teenager leeway to come up with creative ways of handling things by establishing guidelines that offer incentive to think the situation through and practice common sense. Your rules need to inspire your teen to think.

Alert Them Gently to Consequences

For every choice there are consequences—this is true for both you and your teenager. Your responsibility as a parent is to good-naturedly give your teenagers all the information you can about a choice, calmly let them know their options, alert them gently to the consequences, softly guide them as they think it through, and willingly allow them to make a choice. If you're doing this with light-hearted humor and sensitivity, you're doing your part and doing it well.

Teenagers are doing lots of new things, and it's scary because as parents you're financially responsible and emotionally connected. No matter what others say, as a parent you feel that if something goes wrong, it's your fault—you haven't prepared them well enough. You see your teenagers taking risks and making choices and you wonder if they understand fully all the ramifications.

You can make sure your teens have considered all the consequences when you inform them using your best, easy-going style, careful not to imply that you think they haven't thought things through. Cynthia told her son as he was making plans for prom night, "I'm not doing my job if I don't forewarn you." As she listed her concerns, she added, "I'm happy you're willing to listen. I know you've probably already thought of all the repercussions, but I wanted you to know that because you're a teenager, the managers will watch you more closely than other adults and I want you to be aware of that."

While warning your son or daughter, reinforce how much you appreciate being able to talk this matter through. Teenagers are hypersensitive to lecturing, so when you talk with them about the consequences of their actions, they'll be more apt to hear your point if you're treating them as an equal: "Thanks for listening; it helps me know you've thought it through, and I feel better." Remember, it's a conversation, not a monologue. You want them to understand your position without jamming it down their throats, so keep your voice and attitude friendly. When they respond, don't lose your patience or dismiss their thinking. Teenagers often voice strong objections as part of the process, and then end up doing as you requested. When Joe talks with his son about potentially loaded issues, he says to himself, *Don't jump to conclusions . . . don't freak out . . . nothing has happened . . . we're talking.* He reminds his son of the same.

The type of constructive feedback your teenager can use involves looking at the problem, for example, asking, "What might you do differently?" Don't use put-downs; don't be patronizing or condescending. "How can I help you with this situation?" works better than "You really blew it this time."

One mom's slogan for herself is, *No hovering and wringing hands allowed, but gentle hinting and prodding can be helpful.*

Face Problems Squarely

It's cruel to tell your teenager that she can accomplish anything or that he can avoid heartaches and disappointments in life. That just isn't true. But it is true that your teenager has much untapped potential to call on when the crises come. Your son or daughter has deep wells of courage within, and it is up to you to remind them of that in hard times, rather than offer unrealistic pep talks or pie-in-the-sky lectures.

It's best to acknowledge problems. When things are going badly for you or your teenager, admit it by saying, "Life is difficult for us right now." Ignored problems don't go away—they need to be handled directly. Pain does not last forever nor is it unbearable; but avoiding it, sweeping it under the carpet, only makes matters worse.

Positive thinking says you can overcome anything, but there are things in life that are just tragedies; good *can* come out of them, but you must face the crisis squarely. Positive thinking is not enough. Responsible people, regardless of age, design action plans. By your lead, you can teach your teen to be a person of action.

Peg and Jack looked the other way when their thirteen-year-old son, Russ, came home from a seventh-grade party, smelling of booze. At age fourteen, Russ got a ticket for minor-in-possession, and they made excuses. At age fifteen, when Russ was so drunk he could barely walk, they dismissed it as "a stage he's going through." At sixteen, when he was arrested for drunk driving, they grounded him for a month. Jack said, "He'll grow out of it." Peg asked, "What can we do?"

Although it's true that sometimes it is better for you to step back and let you teenager solve his own problems, there are other times when the problem needs your direct action. The first step is to admit, as Jack and Peg finally did, *We've got a problem.* The next step is to decide what action to take. Peg and Jack chose to seek professional guidance.

At seventeen, Russ went to in-patient treatment; now they're all learning to face their problems one day and one step at a time. Problems need to be faced head-on, but they don't have to be solved all at once. Henry Ford said, "Any task, no matter how big, is manageable in small segments." That's how he developed the assembly line. You can solve any problem in manageable sections—one step at a time. There is a proverb that says, *A voyage of a thousand miles begins with one step.* When a problem arises, face it squarely, design an action plan, and get going.

Be Genuine with Praise

I have noticed two things about adults who try to motivate teenagers: (1) the inclination to criticize, correct, chastise, castigate, and point out what the kid is doing wrong; and (2) the tendency toward flowery praise as a way to motivate the teen to continue doing well.

Everyone messes up, but no one likes to have their mistakes pointed out and examined publicly. Some adults mistakenly think that the way to help teens succeed is to draw attention to their flaws so they'll correct them. They think that by pointing out his mistakes, he will avoid making more. However, teenagers are more likely to work on their own shortcomings when given a chance to privately think things over and talk it through with friends. They're less likely to do that if you're complaining, scolding, harping, or reprimanding.

One study found that students who got the poorest grades were the ones who continued to get the most negative reaction from their parents. When they got a bad report card, the parents complained and the grades got worse. The students who improved were the ones whose parents appreciated their effort, expressed moderate concern, and offered to help.

In avoiding criticism, however, be careful not to swing too far the other way. Your teenager is hypersensitive to praise that is disingenuous. Praise is frequently used to manipulate and influence teenagers;

it's a dishonest way of relating. When you flatter your son by saying, "You're always so thoughtful," "You're a great quarterback," "You're a great kid," "You're so smart," or "I can always rely on you," you're pouring on the pressure to live up to the impossible.

Some adults use a strange concoction of praise and criticism to motivate teens. Sean, age fifteen, told me: "When my parents tell me something good about myself, I feel like ducking; I know they're leading up to telling me how I could have done better."

Your role as a parent is to help your teenager grow to his full potential; this is achieved through genuine praise about his behavior, not about his personality. Effective praise acknowledges efforts, achievements, and feelings without making value judgments about character. Telling your teenager, "You're a wonderful person," doesn't describe what you appreciate; it's better to say, "I appreciate your helping out at the last minute."

Anna gave useful praise to the group of teenagers completing an art project: "The mural looks beautiful. It brightens up the school. You worked together and cleaned up your paint. Thanks for pitching in."

When you find yourself wanting to critique your son or daughter, bite your tongue and do a personal inventory. Ask yourself: *What am I trying to accomplish? Is there a better approach?* What specific, genuine praise can you offer in this moment that might help this situation?

Useful praise translates into motivated students who feel capable and valued. Your teenager needs a dose today.

Teach Them to Be Good to Themselves

Teenagers have many temporary setbacks. How they and you deal with these is what makes the difference. Minor setbacks as well as true tragedies happen in everyone's life, but that doesn't mean you have failed or that your teenager is a failure. Strike the word *failure* from your vocabulary and replace it with *setback, mistake, stumbling block, detour,* or *problem in need of a solution.* Then you'll start thinking of yourself and your teenager as problem solvers and you won't be defeated for long.

People who run in marathons all know the experience of "hitting the wall." It's exhausting and disheartening, and the temptation is to quit. We all hit walls in our lives, but if we persist we can persevere and break through. Teens can be their own worse critics, criticizing themselves with negative talk and scrutinizing their looks, their weight, their height, their muscles, their performance. When they do worse than they expect, they worry that they let *you* down and sometimes think, *I must not deserve to be happy, anyway.*

Twins Robyn and Christine tried out for cheerleading, and Robyn didn't make it—the rumor was that she lost by only three votes. Of course, she was devastated. "She cried for three days," her mom, Judy, said. Her parents and sister wanted to take the pain away, but it was beyond their control—there was nothing they could do to change the outcome. It was a complicated situation, for the family felt the excitement of Christine's win and the agony of Robyn's defeat. They tried not to blow it out of proportion and continued with their lives.

One year later when tryouts came again, instead of criticizing herself for her past performance, Robyn found the inner strength to face her fears. She spent hours practicing, competed in front of the student body, and won a spot on the squad. Robyn proved that regardless of how big of a failure you may think of yourself to be, within you is the ability and the power to do whatever you need to do to be happy and successful.

You can teach your teenager to be good to herself even when things are going bad—that much of life depends on circumstances out of her control and therefore say nothing about her self-worth. You can help her focus on what she can do, like Robyn, to achieve her dream.

When you look for the good in all situations, you teach your teenager to see the good in herself. When you act as though everything will be okay, she starts behaving as if it will. So don't make problems bigger by focusing on the negative. Turn adversity into advantage, stumbling blocks into stepping stones.

Give a Choice in Their Day-to-day Lives

Teenagers crave independence. They want to be on their own; they yearn for autonomy and personal freedom. A child who is closely monitored and controlled feels resentful and antagonistic. He is unfriendly and disagreeable toward his parents. At a drop of a hat, he fights with authority figures and won't cooperate with teachers. On the other hand, a teenager who is allowed to be self-sufficient is less hostile toward his parents and other adults. A teenager who is given a voice regarding his daily activities doesn't argue as much.

One of the best ways to give your teenagers independence is to let them have a voice in the day-to-day matters that affect their lives. I have known parents who are still telling their thirteen and fourteen year olds when to go to bed, what foods to eat, and what clothes to wear, yet they're amazed when their child talks back and is sullen, cranky, and disrespectful.

Nancy orchestrated whatever her son did, including making sure he brought flowers to his date's mother. She wanted to be included with his friends, wanted to plan his social events, and desired to spend time together as he was wanting to break away. Whenever his friends were over, she cooked for them and visited with them; and although the friends liked it, he didn't. He wanted to be on his own but she ignored his wishes.

Teens need lots of growing room—time to practice being an adult. If you are always right there giving your opinion, they never quite get the hang of it and end up doubting themselves and making foolish choices.

Don't get overly involved with your teenager's life. If you do, she'll feel smothered, will be irritable, and will move as far away as she can. Right now she needs to be separate and distinct. If you allow this without making her feel guilty, as a young adult she'll reach out to you once more.

Allow Them to Practice Taking Charge

During the teen years, you might sometimes wonder, *Just who is in charge here anyway*? The answer is *you are in charge* (or should be), and although it might not seem so, your teenager still wants it that way. Even as she challenges your authority daily, she unconsciously knows she's not ready to take over all the adult responsibilities. Ideally, the process of growing up is taking charge of more and more things until in adulthood you are a fully autonomous human being. Knowing of what and how much to let your kids take charge is one of the great challenges of parenthood. From deciding when to allow her to cross the street alone, to letting her go away with friends on a trip, you have to use your best instincts to know what to do. Your teenager is so capable that it's easy for you to forget that she needs lots of practice time before she is ready to take on *all* the adult roles.

Your teenager needs to practice being in charge in order to gain confidence. By such practicing, she finds out that she has what it takes to make her life satisfying. By exercising control over his life, your son learns that he is worthwhile and has something to contribute.

This practice is the springboard to adulthood that your teenager needs in order to be convinced that he can manage whatever task or situation he faces. Remind yourself that the more he practices making decisions, the better decision maker he'll become. *What kind of summer job do* I *want? What group of friends do* I *want to hang out with? What classes shall* I *sign up for?*

Your son will be more successful when he knows that if he needs you—even at moment's notice—you're available and willing to step in. As one mother told me, "I let my son be in charge, but I don't let him ruin his life. I step in and back him up when I see that he is getting in over his head."

Your daughter likes to be in charge most of the time, but she also needs you to be there when she needs a rest, feels confused, or when it gets too overwhelming. The wise parent knows he is still in charge, so he doesn't flaunt his power or authority. By understanding the developmental needs of your teenager and with awareness of what you're doing, you're prepared to relinquish more and more of your active control. You're the captain, but you intentionally step aside and let your teenager chart the course. Then if your daughter loses her way, she can come to you, reassured that you will rescue her and sensitively steer her back.

Our sons and daughters may act as though they know more than we do, but our secret is that we know more—even if we don't tell them so.

Trust and Trust Again

Trust is the center of love—without it, your relationship will wither. Trusting your teenager means that whatever he's done, you'll never doubt his goodness. When you trust your teen even when he's behaving untrustworthy, you inspire him to rise to the occasion.

In infancy, your child learns whether he can trust you, and now in adolescence he wants to find out whether you trust him. It's an ongoing process in which he is alert to subtle signals of your trust. You demonstrate your trust by letting her be in charge of her schoolwork, by giving her permission to go places, by not scrutinizing her every move, by letting her choose her dress, her friends, her hair style, by letting her stay home alone, and by avoiding detailed questions.

"My son Jake is right—I don't trust him; he has to show me." It's paradoxical, but when you trust him, even when you're leery, he receives the blessing of your trust and behaves more and more trustworthy.

Trust requires your active involvement. You can't sit back and take a prove-it-to-me attitude. Gayle demonstrated her confidence to fourteen-year-old Sean by expecting him to be in charge of his schoolwork, but she didn't sit back passively and ignore what was going on. She was aware of how he was doing, and when she discovered through observation and progress reports that he was not turning in the English homework, she didn't accuse him of being untrustworthy. Instead, she explored with him what the problem might be. Together, they decided on additional tutoring, and she trusted him to keep the appointments, which he did. Even though he kept the radio blaring when writing his papers, his grades improved.

When your trust is broken, as it probably will be sometime, don't focus on the reasons you can't trust. Instead, face the situation directly and apply some wisdom. Angie's parents found out about the party she threw when they were away. Instead of grounding her, they showed their disappointment, talked about what happened, and gave her the opportunity of redeeming herself by facing the consequences that were appropriately related to the "crime"—cleaning the house the following weekend. The next time they went away, they trusted Angie to again be home alone—and this time, with permission, she invited just one friend.

When trust is broken, trust again, because if you stop, what chance does she have? When you trust and trust again, it pays off, because when she knows you are counting on her to do what she says, she feels inspired to do the right thing. Angie said: "I felt so grateful that my parents still believed in me that I never wanted to break their trust again."

Remember That Teenagers Are Fragile, Too

If fine crystal goblets are handled roughly, without awareness, they'll break. Usually, fine crystal is washed separately and dried carefully. Fine crystal is handled with gentleness—you don't just throw crystal into a dishpan full of dirty old dishes. That's how you have to treat a teenager, as if she were a fine crystal goblet—very fragile. For in a very real way, she is even more delicate than glass.

If you wash crystal when you're in a hurry or if you put it away in a cupboard when you're in a rush, you can nick the rim—a tiny nick, perhaps, maybe not enough to see, but you can feel it when you run your finger across the rim. That's what happens to your child when you treat him roughly, talk with condemning words, or brush him off. When you handle your teenager without gentle care, little nicks happen. They're not even noticeable to the eye, but after a while, those nicks get larger and larger, and they weaken the crystal until one day it cracks. This can happen to your teen's vulnerable self-esteem—a little nick of unawareness can someday cause a major crack and his psyche is shattered beyond repair.

I often ask parents in my classes: "When did you lose your self-confidence?" or "Can you remember when your self-esteem became shaky?" Frequently, they tell me it was during the teen years. Many of them can relate, as if they happened yesterday, incidents that chipped away at their feelings of self-worth.

Although self-esteem is developed in the early years of childhood, kids become vulnerable again during the teen years, particularly about their looks and bodies. Be careful not to tease her about her weight or ridicule him about his physique. What you say can either crush and devastate or restore or uplift. Continual criticism, chiding, or berating from you can impact your child's self-esteem for life.

In early adolescence, almost every child feels down about himself. You need to lift him up with gentle, loving words and take benevolent care of his fragile spirit. Marilyn knew that her twelve-year-old step-daughter, Leilah, was reaching puberty when this event happened: Leilah had always been supremely self-confident with high self-esteem. One day she and her step mom got into an argument, and Leilah was sent to her room to calm down. After about ten minutes or so, Marilyn went up to have a conversation. She was expecting Leilah to attack and thought she'd have to defend herself. Instead, when Marilyn walked in and sat down, Leilah burst out crying, "It's all my fault. I never say the right thing—that's why everyone at school hates me."

When your child is upset, no amount of logic or reasonable advice works as well as cuddling with kindness. When they're not upset, treat them as if God is watching.

Stand Back and Gain Perspective

There are many blessings—sometimes not so obvious—from knowing a teenager, and you may need to stand back to see with a clear perspective. With a teenager at home, you'll have a wonderful opportunity to view the circle of life, to see firsthand the continuity of your life through your son or daughter. When you stand back, you'll catch a reflection of yourself and grasp how your teenager and you are individuals yet spiritually linked through divine destiny.

Perspective comes when you stand back and know that with each problem comes a lesson and a blessing. With perspective, you come to understand that although you're their protector, they teach and guide you too. Sometimes their presence heals the teenage wounds you may have buried and forgotten; other times you'll see how raising them has expanded your capacity to love.

Alice watched her lively sixteen-year-old daughter put on a red sweater to go school and she felt a pang of jealousy as she remembered her own painful teenage years. She was skinny—kids called her "the parking meter"; and she had bad complexion—the kids called her face "the berry patch." Her parents and brothers poked fun and criticized. As a teen, Alice decided that her strategy for coping with life would be to hide, to blend in, to not be seen. For more than twenty years it worked well, she thought, until the day when she burst into tears as she watched her daughter put on the red sweater. She realized that she herself had never worn red because she hadn't wanted to stand out, but now she didn't want to hide anymore.

Mary said that by standing back she finds out how well her son Chuck handles his life, how well he thinks things through, how solid his decisions are. She's learning to give him credit for his life experience. She doesn't have to run the whole show.

With some distance, you'll be able to watch your teenager carve a life that carries the essence of you and is also separate from you. Jean, the mother of two grown sons, says, "When they were young, I was involved in everything they were learning; I was opening the world to them. Now they bring the world to me."

When you stand back, you'll be able to remind yourself that these teenagers, who sometimes seem so impossible, are divine beings of light. We are not so much parents of teens as we're the caretakers of God's teens.

Bravely Let Go

By the time your child reaches adolescence, you'll have a fair amount of experience letting go. And with that experience under your belt, you might be inclined to believe you're adequately prepared for your teen to pull away. You might have heard other parents talking about the traumatic teen years, and although you suspect that it will be challenging to ease your grasp, you feel up to the task. You know you're a sensible, rational, reasonable person. Up to now, you've done a better than average job of parenting, so you feel confident you can handle the grief of letting go.

You're proud to have raised an independent child who can think for herself. You've been enthusiastic as she makes her plans to leave home. Maybe she'll go to college, get a job, get an apartment, get married, or become the chairman of the board. Maybe he'll join the military or play in the NBA, travel through Europe or Asia, become a doctor, a novelist, an engineer.

Whatever the dream, you've both shared in it—you've known from the beginning he would be leaving you at home, striking out on his own. You know you're supposed to let go, yet you don't know how much or when, so you find yourself tangled in a letting-go tug-of-war.

The letting-go tug-of-war starts at thirteen, more or less, and, depending on how hard you're holding on, yanking, pulling, and dragging, it keeps escalating until you give in, give up, and let go. It's the dominant theme, the main motif of the teenage years—she struggles for independence in a zillion and one ways, and you struggle almost as much to keep her close, safe, and protected—after all, she'll always be your baby. In the end, she wins. And although at times you feel like you've lost, friends of mine with kids in their thirties assure me that there are benefits of being on your own—and you won't feel deserted forever.

Letting go takes courage—for both of you. More and more, you feel pangs of sadness as you realize how fast they grow up.

"Parenting never stops—it changes directions and intensity, but it never stops," says Richard. He should know—he raised four teens on his own. Now that they're grown, he's enjoying role reversal. When his twenty-six-year-old son recently took him climbing on Mt. Rainer, Richard was the student, and his son was the teacher.

Stephanie, at age seventeen, reminded her mom directly, "Mom, in a short time I'll be out of here, and you won't be around in person to influence me."

"Do I really need to hear this?"

"Yes, I think you do."

Don't worry—they get homesick and call collect.

Judy Ford, MSW, has been a therapist, public speaker, and human relations consultant for the past twenty years. Her parenting classes, *Parenting with Love and Laughter*, give parents practical tools to use while focusing on the joy of parenting. In addition to her seminars, Judy frequently speaks on the power of love and laughter to enrich both our professional and personal lives. For information on her seminars, write:

P.O. Box 804
Kirkland, WA 98083

Judy Ford and daughter, Manda

If you liked *Wonderful Ways To Love a Teen*, chances are you'll enjoy Conari Press' other titles. Our goal is to publish books that will positively impact people's lives and further our individual and collective growth. Call or write for a free catalog:

Conari Press
2550 Ninth Street, Suite 101
Berkeley, CA 94710
(800) 685-9595

Resource Guide

Adoption Hotline   800-333-6232
Boys Town National Hotline   800-448-3000
        Child Abuse/Missing Children/Mental Health
Child Find of America, Inc.   800-426-5678
Children of the Night Crisis Line   800-551-1300
Children's Rights of America Youth Crisis Hotline   800-442-4673
Family Violence Prevention Fund   800-313-1310
IYG   *Peer counseling for gay, lesbian, and*
        bisexual youth   800-347-8336
National Life Center Hotline/Pregnancy Hotline   800-848-5683
National Runaway Switchboard   800-621-4000
National Youth Crisis Hotline   800-448-4663
Rape, Abuse, and Incest National Network   800-656-4673

NATIONAL DRUG/ALCOHOL & CRIME CLEARINGHOUSES
Alcohol and Drug Helpline   800-821-4357
Cocaine Helpline   800-262-2463
National Clearinghouse for Alcohol and Drug   800-729-6686
    Information   800-729-6686
Juvenile Justice Clearinghouse   800-638-5736

HEALTH & SOCIAL WELFARE
National Health Information Center   800-336-4797
Office of Minority Health Resource Center   800-444-6472
        Spanish- and Asian-speaking operators are available

"Just Say No" International   800-258-2766
        Provides materials, technical assistance, and training to
        help children and teenagers lead drug-free lives.
National Child Safety Council Childwatch   800-222-1464
The Bureau For At-Risk Youth   800-99-YOUTH
        Educational publisher and distributor of programs,
        videos, publications and products for youth-at-risk and
        their caregivers.

National Aids Hotline   800-342-2437
National Aids Hotline (Spanish)   800-344-7432
National Native American Aids Prevention Center   800-283-2437
HIV/Aids Treatment Information Clearinghouse   800-448-0440
National Aids Clearinghouse   800-458-5231
Centers for Disease Control and Prevention National
        Sexual Transmitted Disease Hotline   800-227-8922

AABA—American Anorexia/Bulimia Association   212-891-8686
        A source of public information, support groups, referrals,
        speakers, educational programs, professional training, and a
        quarterly newsletter.
ANAD—National Association of Anorexia Nervosa   708 831-3438
        Distributes listing of therapists, hospitals, and informative
        materials; sponsors support groups, conferences,
        advocacy campaigns, research, and a crisis hotline.

Asthma and Allergy Foundation of America	800-727-8462
Depression Awareness, Recognition, and Treatment	800-421-4211
National Foundation for Depressive Illness	800-245-4381
Juvenile Diabetes Foundation International Hotline	800-223-1138
National Association for Parents of the Visually Impaired	800-562-6265
National Center for Youth with Disabilities	800-333-6293
National Clearinghouse on Family Support and Children's Mental Health	800-628-1696
National Rehabilitation Information Center	800-346-2742
Planned Parenthood Federation of America, Inc.	800-669-0156
Contact Literacy Center/National Literacy Hotline	800-228-8813
Direct. Of American Youth Organizations	800-735-READ
Wave, Inc.	800-274-2005
Youth employment and training	
Women's Sports Foundation	800-227-3988
Young Life International Service Center	719-473-4262